SELF-LOVE:
THE DYNAMIC
FORCE OF SUCCESS

Other Books by Robert H. Schuller

God's Way to the Good Life
Your Future Is Your Friend
Move Ahead with Possibility Thinking

Robert H. Schuller

SELF-LOVE:
THE DYNAMIC
FORCE OF SUCCESS

Introduction by
NORMAN VINCENT PEALE

HAWTHORN BOOKS, INC.
W. Clement Stone, Publisher
NEW YORK

Dedicated to my cherished staff associates

Harold Leestma
Raymond Beckering
Kenneth Van Wyk
Henry Poppen
Frank Boss
Kenneth Narrower
Gene Pearson
Sheldon Disrud
Richard Unfreid

INTRODUCTION

BY DR. NORMAN VINCENT PEALE

The author of this book is a dynamic and creative man who is always searching for truths that can be meaningful in his own life and that he, in turn, can communicate to others. He also believes that when you are confronted with a problem, you can find a way to a solution.

In this book, *Self-Love: The Dynamic Force of Success,* Bob Schuller seeks to show the wellspring of human endeavor. He believes that self-love is a vital force in human existence and that anyone who lacks love of self can never truly live in harmony with the world and realize his or her dreams and goals or enjoy them after attaining them. The self-love he writes about is not a selfish or narcissistic love but the creation and realization of true belief and confidence in yourself as a real person.

A few years ago Bob Schuller wrote a thrilling book called *Move Ahead with Possibility Thinking.* Through this book he was able to inspire and influence many more people than those who fill his church to overflowing every Sunday morning. In it he stated his very strong belief that you must think and act in positive terms in order to realize your ambitions and goals. Yet, there are many persons who seem unable to think and act in this way. Seeking to find the why of their failure to live positively and

7

victoriously, Bob Schuller came to a concept of the importance of self-love.

If you are one of those individuals who continually has doubts about your own ability; if you often wake in the morning hating yourself for lack of achievement; if you don't think much of yourself, you will find here ways to rid yourself of these destructive emotions. You will learn how to substitute for self-dislike the normal self-love, which generates self-belief and self-confidence.

If you are filled with hesitation and doubts, this book will help you find new strength and new hope in dealing with the problems of everyday living. If you do not truly love yourself; if you do not truly believe in yourself; if you do not truly have respect for your own ideas, you will be shown how you can change. You will learn that self-love is important. You will be shown what to do if you do not have it and how to develop this important quality in yourself and in others around you.

The valuable lessons learned in this book can be applied not only in your own life but in the lives of your family, your friends and associates.

The author has the authority to speak about achievement, for he has achieved a great deal in his own life. Given a small sum of money by his denominational headquarters to establish a church in southern California, he has, in a period of twelve short years, constructed a magnificent edifice and one of the great church organizations in the nation. Just recently a thirteen-story Tower of Faith was added to the church building complex, and in it dedicated men and women are counseling others to rebuild shattered lives. Where others doubt or scoff, Bob Schuller always has faith and moves forward with confidence, believing that all good things are possible.

A great deal of the enthusiasm and constructive thinking of this man will be yours after you have read his book. If you will take its message seriously, you will find new horizons opening for you. You will find that you can achieve much that until now you felt was either too difficult or impossible. This book will help you to like yourself better. And liking yourself in a normal, healthy way, you will create a likeable life for yourself.

8

CONTENTS

HOW THIS BOOK WILL HELP YOU LOVE YOURSELF SO THAT YOU WILL REALLY COME ALIVE

After publication of *Move Ahead with Possibility Thinking,* I was pleased to receive many letters from readers who expressed appreciation for what I had written. However, I also heard from others who wrote that they had tried to practice Possibility Thinking but inevitably ended by thinking negatively. I realized that there are many people who seem unable to break the impossibility thinking chain that imprisons their spirits in tombs of gloom.

Why is it, I asked myself, that some people read books that show the way of positivism and still remain negative. Why do these people find it difficult to approach life's problems with the attitude that they can conquer them? Why, like so many other individuals I have met, did they instinctively reach for the "it can't be done" or "it won't work" approach to every challenge?

SOMETHING GREATER THAN POSSIBILITY THINKING

After much thought and questioning I came to the realization that those who think negatively simply do not think highly of themselves.

Every negative thinker I have ever met distrusts himself, belittles himself, and downgrades himself.

This lack of self-worth lies at the root of almost every one of our personal problems. After the Holy Bible, this book might be the greatest book you'll ever read if it leads you

11

to make life's most exciting and constructive discovery: your own latent self-worth, which is something greater than possibility thinking.

Once when I challenged an impossibility thinker to become a possibility thinker, his answer provided a revelation. "It's not worth the effort," he said. As he spoke, I studied his eyes, the window of his soul, and knew he didn't mean it. He really meant, "I'm not worth it." I dropped the idea of converting him to possibility thinking. Instead I went to work to build up in his mind a picture of his enormous worth as a person. Then, little by little, when he began to stop hating himself and started liking himself, he came alive. He became a possibility thinker.

DISCOVER WHAT A WONDERFUL PERSON YOU REALLY ARE—OR CAN BE

No matter what has happened in your life you are *not* "a *complete* failure," "a *hopeless* sinner," "a *total* washout." After twenty years in the field of people-counseling I have heard that exaggerated, distorted, destructive lie repeated many hundreds of times. In almost every instance I was able to see and point out worthwhile qualities in the person who was condemning himself unfairly, unreasonably, unlovingly. In this book you will come to see that there are vast undamaged areas in every human life.

A REBIRTH OF SELF-WORTH AWAITS YOU

When that happens you will be
    poised instead of tense,
    confident instead of confused,

bold instead of timid,
enthusiastic instead of bored,
successful instead of failing,
energetic instead of fatigued,
agreeable instead of cantankerous,
positive instead of negative
self-forgiving instead of self-condemning
self-respecting instead of self-disgusting.

WHY I BELIEVE I HAVE THE ANSWERS YOU SEEK

I know this book can help you because the principles have been tested time and again in the laboratory of human experience. For twenty years as a pastoral counselor I have advised thousands of worshipers in the nation's most populous state. I speak to nearly 6,000 people every Sunday. People often bring their problems to a pastor when they dare not go elsewhere. Many fear psychiatry and the psychiatrist. They mistakenly assume that people will view them strangely if it is known they are under analysis. Frequently, their minister, priest or rabbi will refer them to a psychiatrist after reassuring them that such fears are unjustified. Individuals with every conceivable kind of human problem have come to me for help. I have yet to see a troubled person who, when he acquired a warm and affectionate feeling for himself, was not vastly improved. My spiritual therapy has consisted especially in building an inspiring self-regard into human lives. The principles I use are in this book. From these experiences I am offering something you really need and want. I believe absolutely—"self-disgust leads to self-rust," but "self-esteem puts you on the beam!"

13

THIS BOOK IS FOR MANY PEOPLE

This book is not only for people who suffer from lack of self-regard. It is also for the self-confident. Even the self-respecting person riding high with success suffers occasional disappointment or realizes that someday he must step down for others. What happens then? How will you be able to love yourself if you turn into what you may regard as a "has-been"? You'll find many helpful answers in this book—I guarantee it!

This book is for the financially successful as well as for the poor. Surprisingly the suicide rate is higher among the more affluent than among those in lower income brackets.

If you belong to an oppressed minority group, this book can show you what you really need to get what you want no matter who you are or where you live.

This book is for people with problems. It is imporatnt to understand how a birth of self-worth is necessary before one can rise above difficulties.

This book can provide guidance for the teacher. The teacher's greatest success comes when he inspires a student to believe in the unlimited potential that lies deep within his being.

This book can provide answers for the clergyman. If your job is to save souls, you can do this when you liberate them from the sin of self-degradation and lift them to salvation and self-esteem. Come to the understanding that self-will is sin, self-love is salvation!

This book can throw light on improved management-employee relations. The manager who learns that his worker's greatest need is a sense of self-dignity will find a happier employee. Then watch the efficiency, cooperation and productivity mount!

This book can be used by politicians. Those who realize that self-dignity is the highest human value, that it rests on something more than handouts, and that every man has a right to self-love, will become progressive, pacesetting, positive helpers of humanity.

IT'S UP TO YOU TO GIVE YOUR SELF-RESPECT A BOOST

Other people will not respect you if you don't respect yourself. If you run yourself down, you'll soon have those who would boost you believing you are right and they are wrong. You need all the encouragement you can get in life. You will learn how to become your own best friend. We need all the friends we have to carry on cheerfully when the going is rough. So you can't afford to lose yourself as a friend. Hope, faith, love, optimism and cheerfulness will begin to rise within you, and you'll like yourself even more. Others will naturally like that new person. Strength will grow in you. Success will follow.

TO LOVE YOURSELF IS TO BE TRULY RELIGIOUS

It's not a sin to experience a wonderful feeling of self-affection. It *is* a sin not to love what God loves. True religion teaches that God loves every person. No person will love God so long as he fails to love himself. Jesus Christ had this remarkable perception when he offered the eleventh com-

15

mandment, Thou shalt love the Lord thy God and thy neighbor *as thyself.*

A member of my church who was a millionaire lost his entire fortune. Worse yet—he lost all of his self-respect. As his spiritual counselor, aiming to rebuild his broken spirit, I asked, "Do you love God?" "Yes" was the reply.

"Do you love yourself?"

"No."

"Then you do not really love God, for God lives within you too," I said.

He understood the fact that if you say you love God and do not love yourself, you are not being honest! Understanding this he decided to learn to love himself. When he succeeded, his earlier "love of God" turned into a really powerful belief in God. So strong was this belief that he started over again and is today moving ahead rapidly.

YOU ARE GOING TO BE A DIFFERENT PERSON AFTER READING THIS BOOK

That's safe to say. You will be a different person next week from the one you are today. All of us are constantly changing, sometimes for the better, sometimes for the worse. You change for the better when you feed your mind and body healthy food. Your hardest task will be to believe— really believe—"I am a better person than I think I am."

You *can* become a wonderful, worthwhile person. Can you believe this? If you can, then I can promise you—you have some great days ahead of you.

16

I

WHAT YOU REALLY WANT IN LIFE— MAN'S ULTIMATE WILL

"I feel a restiveness in man," Dr. Robert Ardrey has written, "a dissatisfaction of a universal sort—the average human being, as I judge it, is uneasy. He is like a man who is hungry, gets up at night, opens the refrigerator door and doesn't exactly see what he wants because he doesn't know what he wants. He closes the door and goes back to bed." *

Not knowing what we really want, we go through life with a strange inner hunger unsatisfied. It's something like having a holiday without knowing exactly what you want to do, where you want to go, or how you want to spend your limited time. When you finally decide what you want to do, and where to go, it's too late.

A little boy was given a quarter to spend in any way he chose. Walking through a toy store, the coin burning in his hand, he first fondled a book, then a plastic car, then a bag

* The Territorial Imperative.

of balloons. The more he looked and touched, the more confused he became over how to spend his quarter. He just couldn't make up his mind. Finally he bought a whistle. He left the store happily blowing the whistle, thrilling to its music. By the time he was halfway home, he had grown tired of its sound. Finally he broke into tears and cried, "Why did I buy a whistle? I didn't want a whistle after all!" He had spent his money on something he only *thought* he wanted.

There are many people traveling through life like this. They come mournfully to the end of their lives, unsatisfied, unfulfilled, sadly suspecting that they never found what they really wanted.

What do you want more than anything else in the world? What is the basic, driving force in life? The chances are you don't really know the answers to those all-important questions. Philosophers, religious leaders, psychologists and anthropologists have probed for centuries into the nature of man in an attempt to find the answer. Let's take a quick look at some of their conclusions.

SURVIVAL

"Man's basic urge is survival," the anthropologist Jean Pierre Hallet told me. Many will agree. Unless you are mentally ill, you want to survive. The *will to live* is a fantastically powerful drive, but survival is not in itself the greatest or the only motivating force. Legions of sane people have rationally chosen to risk death to reach goals they valued more highly than life itself. Love of country has stirred millions to march off to war ready and willing to make the supreme sacrifice. Millions of sensible human beings have chosen to die in dignity rather than to live in shame.

18

THE EXPERIENCE OF PLEASURE

The *will to pleasure,* according to Sigmund Freud, explains the basic deep-seated wants of human beings. Beyond a doubt, the will to pleasure is a very real and very powerful force behind human behavior. On the other hand, men and women by the millions have been known to forsake physical pleasure in favor of work, love, religion or war. Man craves something much deeper than pleasure. The appetites of the eye, the stomach, the ear and the sex organs can be satisfied and yet the human spirit hungers for something beyond those immediate satisfactions.

THE FEEL OF POWER

The great psychiatrist Alfred Adler suggested that the *will to power* explains everything. The desire to be in control, the craving to be king, the exhilaration of being able to command—all illustrate clearly man's drive for power. The bloody pages of history offer horrendous evidence that man will kill, cheat, lie and betray his own soul in his pursuit of power.

Yet power does not produce ultimate satisfaction. On the contrary, power often produces enormous anxiety and feelings of insecurity. The man on the top is the man who is shot at, threatened and challenged by those who seek his office. The economic, military, technological and intellectual powers of this country are without equal. Yet all this power fails to command complete respect from other nations. To possess power without respect leads to futility and frustration.

I submit that neither the will to survival nor the will to pleasure nor the will to power is at the root of human motives and actions. To cite any of these forces as the basic urge of man is like mistakenly considering the swirling streams on the surface of a river as the major current in that body of water. While the surface waters of human emotion swirl and distract, in the depths below there lies a powerful primeval urge that is hidden from view and must be discovered before we can accomplish our real goals.

Let us look at some other theories about the basic drives of mankind.

MEANING IN LIFE

Viktor Frankl detects a deep and powerful undercurrent in human motivational forces when he suggests that the *will to meaning* is the ultimate will of man. With perception, he has pointed out that man is able to achieve mental and emotional equilibrium when he sees a meaning in his life experience. This may explain why some people are able to achieve peace of mind in the midst of enormous suffering and frustration. They can see meaning in it all. But deep down inside we seek something beyond meaning.

THE CREATIVE FORCE

Every human being finds satisfaction when he sees the results of his creativity. So some human beings deprive themselves of pleasure, power, even love to pursue a vastly rewarding creative enterprise in some lonely attic. It is obvious that many people suffer from frustration and subsequent anxieties because they are performing a menial task and their latent creative potential finds no way of expression. Indeed, creativity is a strong subsurface current in man. But the craving to be creative is not the basic force we are seeking.

SELF-LOVE

I strongly suggest that *self-love* is the ultimate will of man —that what you really want more than anything else in the world is the awareness that you are a worthy person. It is the deepest of all the currents which drive man onward, forward and upward. All other drives—pleasure, power, love, meaning, creativity—are symptoms, expressions or attempts to fulfill that primal need for personal dignity. Examine the will to pleasure, for instance. Ask yourself this question: What's the difference between pleasure and labor? That which is fun for you may be work for someone else.

I have always enjoyed deep-sea fishing. One day in the waters off Catalina I hooked a huge fish. What a struggle until I brought him close enough for the skipper to gaff him. I was exhausted! But I was also exhilarated. Now suppose this was the way I earned my living—day after day. This "work" would have left me tired and exhausted, eager to see the end of the day. Why did I find the experience pleasurable? Because I was able to escape completely from my everyday problems. Work is fun when it is exciting enough or distracting enough to make us forget ourselves completely. At that time I was unhappy with myself for being overweight, so I enjoyed the adventure of escaping from myself. For millions of people the pursuit of pleasure is often a neurotic attempt to escape from the tension of consciously living with an unattractive self.

The quest for self-love sheds light on many sexual adventures. For many people sex is a clumsy attempt to build

21

self-love. The teen-age girl surrenders to the aggressive male for fear that she may lose him if she doesn't go "all the way." A quick analysis might indicate that it is a fear of rejection that motivates this sexual promiscuity. Deeper analysis would show that she unconsciously assumes that if she is rejected she will hate herself. How can she love herself if the boys don't want her?

It has been observed that the wandering male in his forties who moves from one affair to the next is driven by a deep insecurity. At the expense of another person's dignity, he tries to prove to himself that he's "quite a man!" He fails to comprehend that self-love is assaulted more than it is strengthened in any affair that treats individuals as so many "things."

At the same time this same man may be making the tragic mistake of assuming that (1) if he achieves power and influence, people will know him; (2) if they know him, they might love him; (3) if they love him, then he will love himself; (4) if he is in a position of power, he will be able to compel people to respect him. He doesn't realize that power is not what he really wants—but rather, real self-love. Where the will to pleasure is often a neurotic escape from facing oneself, the will to power is frequently a crude attempt to prove "I'm a great guy."

This explains the behavior of a man I shall call George Smith, who had a strong drive to be the president of his company. He worked hard and struggled and after many years built a successful national sales organization. He was made president. He was now at the top! He was excited. Because of this excitement he thought he had achieved happiness.

Then things began to fall apart. Business fell off. First it

22

was necessary to close the New York office, then the Chicago office. As his empire crumbled, he saw himself losing the entire business he had worked for years to build. The terrible day came when he had to close his last office.

Here is how George Smith tells his story: "I locked the door of my office. Never had I felt so low as I did when I turned my back on the door of my broken dreams. I walked slowly to the parking lot, got into my car and headed for home. Oh, God, it was all I had left! I stepped into the house. I expected to hear my wife call out, 'Is that you dear?' I heard nothing. I walked to the kitchen and found a note: 'I've gone shopping. Be home late.' I sank into a chair, a crushed human being.

"Suddenly the door opened. It was my little girl, home from school. She put her lunch box on the table, spotted me and called, 'Daddy! How come you're home so early?' I answered, "Well, honey, Daddy is changing jobs, but let's not talk about it now. Okay?' Then my daughter jumped on my lap, hugged me tight around the neck, pressed her soft and warm face against my face, and gave me the warmest, sweetest kiss, saying, 'Oh, Daddy, I love you so much!' That did it. I really cracked up. My lips quivered. She said, 'What's wrong, Daddy?' I said, 'Nothing, honey, nothing at all. There's absolutely nothing wrong!'

"And I really meant it. In that moment I discovered that I had what I really wanted. Suddenly my whole life unfolded before me: a young fellow that wanted to be a great success in order to be recognized, in order to feel important, in order to be loved, in order to really respect myself! Well, I had what I wanted. It was here in my lap! I was loved. And in loving and being loved, I found my sense of self-worth, self-respect and self-dignity."

So it is the will to dignity, not the will to power, that man seeks. Man is a dignity seeker—not a status seeker. He makes a terrible mistake if he thinks that status will insure self-worth.

This may explain why a very successful "status seeker" resigned his job soon after he arrived at the top. "It did not satisfy me; in fact, it made me ill. I had to pretend to love people I didn't and couldn't love. I had to overlook things that I knew were wrong. I had to surrender moral and ethical principles to get to the top and to stay at the top. In my happiest moments, I felt the exhilaration of being a big wheel! But I was not satisfied! I was not satisfied because I could not respect myself for what all this was doing to my sense of values. So I quit."

Of course! He quit because he learned that he was not getting what he thought he wanted. He did not get what he wanted because he did not know that what he really wanted was exalted self-esteem.

Even the will to love is a clever mask hiding the deeper and undetected will to self-love. As infants we learn that we love and are usually loved in return, which leaves us with a wonderful feeling of well-being. We fail to perceive that this sense of well-being is really an experience of self-love. So we go through life driven by the compulsion to love—unaware that what we really seek is not love as an end in itself, but as food to nourish our self-love. Again we discover, early in life, that a wonderful feeling of well-being sweeps over us when we love other persons. We fail to analyze our feelings precisely enough if we stop short of labeling that sense of well-being what it really is—self-love. So the will to love and to be loved is a compulsion either to share our strong self-love or to support our shaky self-love.

Even the will to meaning, under critical analysis, will often prove to be an expression of the will to self-love. If we see no other meaning in our existence, no meaning in our suffering, no meaning in our achievement, no meaning in our love, we will not be able to live with ourselves. On the other hand, we can tolerate unbelievable suffering if we can see some good that will come out of it. We feel we are worthwhile when we see meaning bestowing dignity on our troubles. Meaning is empty unless it feeds and nourishes your self-esteem.

What about the will to creativity? A watchmaker who constructs a watch is able to look at his creation and see himself in the work materialized before him. When his creation is excellent, this shows that he is a worthwhile person. So the will to creativity is really a constructive and wholesome attempt to satisfy the deeper ultimate will—self-love.

MAN IS A PLEASURE-SEEKING, POWER-SEEKING, LOVE-SEEKING, MEANING-SEEKING, CREATIVITY-SEEKING ANIMAL BECAUSE HE IS FIRST AND FOREMOST A DIGNITY-SEEKING CREATURE.

You are on the road to emotional, mental and spiritual health when you discover that what you really want more than anything else in life is neither survival nor pleasure, nor power, nor love, nor meaning. What you really want is to be able to know and appreciate yourself.

THE UNIVERSAL WILL TO SELF-LOVE

This will to self-love is universal. It shows its disguised, often distorted and disfigured face in all ages, among all races and nationalities. The Oriental must save face. Primitive tribes stoutly support their pride with warfare and the adornment of ears, lips and body with self-love–feeding embellishments. It explains why the Yanks are cocky; the English snobbish; the French haughty; the Spanish arrogant; the Dutch and Germans stubborn; the Irish fiery; the Scandinavians determined; the Greeks, Italians, Slovaks and native American Indians proud; and the Jews (according to their own chronicler) stiff-necked.

Desmond Morris, in his book *The Naked Ape,* is awe-stricken by the profound question: "Why is Man—of all the primates—hairless?" If the pelts of all the primates were stretched out in a row, Mr. Morris reminds us, one pelt would stand out with startling uniqueness. It has no hair! Why? How did the Homo sapiens get so bald?

A far more important observation might be made if we placed all of the primates, alive and squirming, in a row of cages. One would note that one primate stands out from all the rest! One primate is driven by a hunger for self-esteem. Why? How did the Homo sapiens develop such a strong will to self-love?

I asked Viktor Frankl: "If it is true that all living organisms have evolved from a slimy amoeba in a swampy pool, and if the human being is the highest form of this purely natural evolution, can you tell me how the human being ever evolved into a creature that demands dignity? Why, of all organisms, does the human being have this craving for dignity, self-respect and self-love?"

"The answer to that question," he replied, "is one I really don't know."

Abraham Kaplan, Chairman of the Philosophy Department of the University of Michigan, was giving the Adolph Meyer lecture at the annual meeting of the American Psychiatric Association in Los Angeles. In his message he challenged these psychiatrists (including a few nonpsychiatrists such as myself): "Oftentimes it seems to me that psychiatrists have a way of saying, 'I don't know,' when actually they are dodging their commitments. Cowardice is disguised as humility. You don't want to admit it, but the real truth is that the human being is this way because there is a God and we are the reflections of God, just as surely as the moon is the reflection of the sun."

MAN—THE GREAT SELF-LOVE–SEEKER

Man is the great self-love–seeker. Why?

Carlyle came close to the answer when he wrote, "Man was made for greatness!" Perhaps the Psalmist had the answer when he wrote, "Man was made in the image of God, just a little lower than the angels."

Suddenly the Holy Bible seems logical and very scientific. According to the Bible, the first human being was created a little like God: with the urge to be creative, a desire to act gloriously and a compulsion to live life on a grand scale. So God placed man in charge of God's ordered creation, to rule, exercise dominion and be the great decision-making creature. Man was a supreme display of dignity incarnate! He was the star of God's creation!

So the urge for greatness, the compulsion to create, the passion for excellence, the desire for recognition, the discontent with imperfection, the demand for personal freedom, the need to give and receive love, even the desire to rule and dominate—all originate with our ancestral divine heritage when God made man to be great, glorious and perfectly proud.

27

When a man senses that he is near greatness, at the beginning of something big, at the edge of glory, at the brink of success, on the stairway to stardom, his heart beats fast and his blood stirs, his pulse pounds with happy anticipation! For he was born for greatness!

We sense that we were born for something bigger and better than we know today. We keep moving restlessly onward and upward, seeking a dignity we instinctively know is our heritage.

Man is unique in that he is a self-love–seeking animal.

Self-love is, or should be, the basic will in human life. Unfortunately, civilization has so clouded and obscured this motivational force that we must explore our inner self to uncover it. We even have to learn what it really is.

II

SELF-LOVE—HIGH HAT OR HALO?

Self-love—what is it?

Self-love can best be defined by those who have experienced it. You will better understand self-love when you, yourself, have savored this deeply satisfying emotional state. Then you will find that you can write your own definition in concrete terms. Until then, perhaps some of the experiences of others will point the way.

Let us begin to discover the meaning of self-love by first revealing what self-love is not.

SELF-LOVE IS NOT ARROGANCE

The haughty or arrogant person is really suffering from a tragic lack of healthy self-love. It is well recognized that the person who displays a superior attitude toward others is in fact using his braggadocio to cover up a deep-rooted inferiority complex. Egotism is a breezy symptom of a trembling insecurity. Exaggeration is also born of insecurity.

Racial arrogance (prejudice) is essentially rooted in a deep insecurity—the need to feel superior to others. Then, there is the fear of losing one's extended identity through intermarriage. Man looks upon his offspring and his offspring's offspring as extensions of himself. The prospect that his children or his grandchildren might conceivably have a different-colored skin or differently shaped eyes instills in the subconscious a fear of a dissolution of his distinctive identity. What he really fears is the loss of something that he believes is distinctively himself.

The self-confident person who enjoys a healthy self-love never demonstrates a "high-hat" attitude. He may be ebullient, effervescent, intensely enthusiastic, but he is never condescending in his attitude toward people of lesser achievement. A self-loving person never considers another human being as "lower" than himself—only different.

SELF-LOVE IS NOT TO BE CONFUSED WITH NARCISSISM

Remember the mythological Greek Narcissus, who looked upon himself in the mirroring waters and was enamored of the beauty of his own face and figure. The narcissistic person is one who is enthralled with his own appearance. Enraptured by the shape of an eye, profile, hair style, shape of nose, the narcissist is often mistakenly analyzed as a self-loving person. "Boy, does he think he's handsome!" or "She's pretty but does she know it" are typical of the remarks made about the narcissist. In reality, narcissism, like arrogance, is caused by a lack of true self-love.

I recall a young teen-ager who grew his hair in long curls. His parents objected vigorously. They finally forced a showdown and demanded that his hair be cut. The next day their son ran away from home. The parents were shocked. What they failed to understand was that for this young man long hair was his narcissistic object. I knew the boy well. He was immature, an insecure adolescent exercising narcissism as a counterfeit for self-love. Narcissism is not authentic self-love, but a symptom of the pitiful lack of it. Actually, the person who has achieved a mature sense of self-love is quite unimpressed with his physical, organic self.

SELF-GLORIFICATION IS NOT SELF-LOVE

An analyst might very well have reason to suspect a lack of adequate and mature self-love in the person who always wears his medals on his chest, adorns his office with all of his awards and trophies, and gives evidence of an extreme self-glorification. This kind of braggart, the blow-your-own-horn person, is basically insecure. When a truly secure person receives the plaudits of his peers, he sincerely dismisses the honors as quickly as possible. His awareness of self-worth does not need these glorifying reassurances.

ABOVE ALL—SELF-LOVE IS NOT SELF-WILL

Self-will is also an aggressive expression of the inner lack of self-assurance. Self-will is expressed in the attitude, "I want what I want when I want it." This is another hallmark of emotional insecurity. It is the child ego state in action. Self-will, born of insecurity, nourished by a lack of self-confidence, plants its aggressive horns in the mind of a per-

31

son who has never really achieved self-love. Self-will is that unpleasant distinctive quality in the human soul that all religions seek to curb, cure or convert. A man becomes a religious being when self-will is displaced by self-love.

WHAT THEN IS SELF-LOVE?

Self-love is a crowning sense of self-worth. It is an ennobling emotion of self-respect. It is a divine awareness of personal dignity. It is what the Greeks called reverence for the self. It is an abiding faith in yourself. It is sincere belief in yourself. It comes through self-discovery, self-discipline, self-forgiveness and self-acceptance. It produces self-reliance, self-confidence and an inner security, calm as the night.

Self-love is expressed and understood in many ways.

SELF-LOVE IS BEING TRUSTED

For Lord Shaftesbury it was an experience at a London traffic crossing. A trembling little girl, not daring to cross the street alone, looked up at him and asked, "Please, sir, will you help me cross the street?" Later Shaftesbury said, "That little girl's faith in me was the greatest compliment I ever had in my life."

SELF-LOVE IS KNOWING YOU ARE WANTED

The real joy of self-love that I experience does not come from personal success as much as it does from knowing that I am needed.

Recently I returned from an extended trip to the East

Coast, making appearances on television and radio to promote my previous book, *Move Ahead with Possibility Thinking*. When I arrived at Garden Grove I was informed that Melvin Payne, a member of my church for almost thirteen years, had died. I immediately drove to his small house to call on his widow.

I rang the doorbell. "Who is it?" a tired voice called out.

"Reverend Schuller," I replied.

"Oh, please come in!"

I opened the door and saw the elderly woman rise wearily from her overstuffed chair. With the faltering step of an old and saddened woman, Mrs. Payne walked slowly toward me, both arms outstretched, eyes glistening. Swiftly I embraced her like a strong son embracing a mother. Her soft hair brushed my cheek and she said, "Oh, Reverend Schuller, I am so glad you got home in time for Melvin's service."

In that brief moment of time I experienced self-love. It was an exalted moment of realized self-worth.

SELF-LOVE IS GIVING YOUR LOVE TO SOMEONE WHO NEEDS YOU

I think of a husband and wife who have three healthy daughters and a young son who is a mongoloid. "We love all our children equally. But we *enjoy* our son the most," the father told me. "Perhaps it is because we know the others can get along on their own. But we know that he needs us. And we all need to be needed. When I come home from work, even though I have accomplished great things in my profession of engineering, I pick up my little boy with the slanted eyes and feel his thin arms curl around my neck. I hold him tight and in that supreme moment I know that I

am a very important person to him. In that divine second I
have an enormous and overwhelming sense of self-worth."

SELF-LOVE IS BEING TRUE TO YOUR
HIGHEST IDEALS

A young man shared this story with me. "I was bored one
night and went to a neighborhood bar. I met this chick and
we started drinking. She was lonely. I was bored. I was un-
married. She was divorced. 'Let's go to Las Vegas,' she suggested. I looked at the hungry invitation in her sultry eyes
and immediately put my glass down, paid the bartender,
took her arm and headed for her car. She snuggled warmly
and hungrily close to me. We roared through the night with
visions of a hot bed in a Vegas motel. For some strange
reason that I cannot explain, I was suddenly gripped by the
thought that this was a pretty cheap thing for me to do. I
found myself mentally torn at the sexual compulsion to 'shack
up' with this barfly for whom I had no respect whatsoever.
At the same time, glancing at the rear-view mirror, I saw
my own eyes. They were the eyes of a potentially wonderful
person. I was beginning to feel the disgust and self-loathing
that I had known on more than one previous occasion after
indulging in a depersonalizing sexual escapade. I pulled over
to the shoulder of the road and stopped the car. 'What are
you doing?' she asked.

" 'I'm getting out,' I answered abruptly. 'It's your car. Go
on to Vegas if you want to. I don't care what you do. I'll
thumb a ride back.' I slammed the door shut and watched
as she angrily spun the wheels in the gravel and roared
furiously away. I stood there alone in the night on a lonely
stretch of desert road. Suddenly I felt ten feet tall! I never

felt so good in my life! I felt like a triumphant general re-
turning victoriously from a proud battle. That was my moment of self-love."

SELF-LOVE IS THE CROWNING EMOTION THAT YOU FEEL WHEN YOU KNOW YOU ARE BEING HONEST

I asked a Mexican-American, "Have you ever experienced
self-love?" He unfolded this story.

"Once, when I was a young boy, I stole a three-dollar
piece of jewelry. I brought it home. My dad saw it and
asked, 'What did you pay for it?' 'Nothing,' I said. He just
looked at me. I felt his honest fatherly spirit soak into me
and I began to hate myself for stealing it. 'What should I do?'
I asked. 'Take it back to the store,' he advised. I went to the
store, walked trembling to the counter and told the jeweler
what I had done. Before he could answer, I reached into my
pocket and took out the ring with three dollars to pay for it.
I still remember the wonderful feeling I had when my hand
went into my pocket and felt the ring—and that wonderful
feeling when I laid that ring on the glass counter and put
three dollars next to it."

SELF-LOVE IS DISCOVERING THE GREATNESS SLUMBERING DEEP WITHIN YOU

On one occasion, while traveling from California to Iowa,
we watched the endless acres of fertile Iowa farmland move
past our car window. It is a majestic sight to see the good
earth bearing a heavy harvest of grain and corn. Not an

acre is wasted. Every piece of land is put to good use. After the fruitful plains we reached the bleak and barren foothills of the great Rocky Mountains. These rugged peaks greet the traveler like granite sentinels standing guard at the gateway to the Pacific. We began to climb the twisting road that winds like a snake up the hillside. Finally we reached a point where we could look to the west and see the beautiful but unproductive mountains and to the east where unfolding below on the endless plains was the rich farmland with little lakes and rivers shimmering in the scene. What a contrast! I stopped for gas and, pointing to the mountains, made the mistake of saying to the station attendant, "What a lot of worthless land!" That fine young man whirled around, looked at me with fire in his eyes and firmly corrected me with these words, "That is *not* wasteland. There are minerals in those rocks, and there may be oil. We believe there is uranium too. We just haven't found it yet."

Men and women also have untapped possibilities to achieve success in life where often, at first glance, it appears there are none. "You are the salt of the earth. . . . You are the light of the world," Jesus Christ said to the motley crowd gathered on the mountain to hear Him preach. "You are somebody!"

There was one broad-shouldered, rough-faced, fiery-eyed, uneducated fisherman who drank in every word that Jesus uttered. Peter was a self-belittler. "I'm not much. Just an old fisherman. I haven't gone to school like some of these folks. I have an awful temper, and I'm not handsome." But Peter listened—Peter believed—and Peter arrived! Jesus Christ teaches that regardless of our past experiences or our present position, our future possibilities are tremendous if we will learn to believe in our potential which may be hidden. YOU

36

HAVE NO IDEA WHAT A TREMENDOUS PERSON YOU CAN BE IF
YOU WILL ONLY BELIEVE IN YOURSELF.

SELF-LOVE IS BEING PROUD OF WHO
AND WHAT YOU ARE

Champion boxer Archie Moore has been redeeming dozens
of young lives through his program which he called "ABC—
Any Boy Can." He says, "By teaching our youth, black,
white, yellow and red, what dignity is, what self-respect is,
what honor is, I have been able to obliterate or reduce
juvenile delinquency in several areas. ABC programs are
now operating in San Diego and Vallejo, California, and a
number of other cities are interested in establishing similar
programs."

"Be proud of your ancestry. Be proud of your country!" is
the premise on which Archie Moore's ABC program starts.
Instead of stimulating resentment, such an attitude inspires
goodwill. Rather than generating a defensive stance, it inspires enthusiasm. This spirit and quality have done wonders
for Archie Moore himself. "I'll fight the man who calls me
an 'Uncle Tom,'" Archie Moore has stated. "I have broken
bread with heads of state, chatted with Presidents and traveled all over the world. I was born in a ghetto, but I refused
to stay there. *I am a Negro and proud to be one. I am also
an American and I'm proud of that.*

"The young people of today think they have a hard lot.
They should have been around in the forties when I was
coming up in St. Louis. We had no way to go. But a lot of
us made it. I became light heavyweight champion of the
world. A neighbor kid down the block, Clark Terry, became
one of the most famous jazz musicians in the world. There

were doctors, lawyers and chiefs who came out of that ghetto. One of the top policemen in St. Louis came from our neighborhood. We made it because we had a goal and we were willing to work for it."

In a recent speech Mr. Moore said, "If any boy can, surely any man can. I want to take teams of qualified people, top men in their fields, to the troubled areas of our cities. I know that the people who participate in riots are misguided rather than mad. If some bigot can misguide, then I can guide. I spent too much of my life building what I've got to put it to the torch just to satisfy some ancient hatred of a man who beat my grandfather. Those men are long dead. Do we have to choke what could be a beautiful garden with weeds of hate? I say NO! And I am now getting ready to start 'Operation Gardener,' to pull the 'weeds of hate' and plant the 'seeds of self-respect.' "

So self-love is rising above embarrassment about your origins. It is living beyond humiliation which someone may try to impose. Self-love is an awareness that you can be a very fine person—no matter what some people may say or think.

SELF-LOVE IS EXPERIENCING GOD AT WORK IN YOU AND THROUGH YOU

Dr. Louis Evans has told this story of a visit to a mission station in Korea. A medical missionary friend invited him to witness an operation involving major surgery in a makeshift tent in an out-of-the-way area. The heat was stifling. The odors were oppressive. Hour after grueling hour the steady, calm, determined surgeon worked on an old peasant woman. After seven hours, the doctor stood up, drew back his mask and sighed, "Well, the job is done, Lou." Together they returned to the modest missionary's office where Dr. Evans asked, "I'm curious, how much do you get paid out here in Korea for an operation like this?"

The surgeon answered, "To begin with, I get this," and he picked up a dented copper coin. "This poor old woman came in here some time ago with this old coin and said, 'Doctor, do you suppose this would pay for the operation?' I answered, 'It so happens that it is just enough.' So to begin with, I got this piece of change." Sitting down, with a warm moisture filling his learned eyes, the dedicated minister of healing added, "But most of all, Lou, what I get is the wonderful feeling that for seven hours Christ is living in these ten fingers! I have the priceless awareness that these hands become the hands of Jesus Christ healing one of His children."

That, too, is a manifestation of self-love. Experiencing Christ living in you and loving people through your life will make you believe in yourself and enjoy true self-love.

So real self-love is not man's high hat—it is man's halo! No wonder true self-love brings that satisfaction which promotes belief in self, which in turn makes you realize that you *can* do what you set out to do.

III

LOVE YOURSELF—OR YOU WILL BE YOUR OWN WORST ENEMY

"What's the matter with him, anyway?"

"I tell you, he can be a queer duck sometimes. I wish I could understand him."

"I don't see why I'm always getting so tired out—I'm not working that hard."

How often are statements like these made every day in every community where human beings live and work.

We gain an enlightened understanding of our own problems as well as new insight into our problem-plagued acquaintances when we realize that a lack of self-love is the sick root responsible for nearly all problems in the human personality.

Come along with me and meet that nasty neighbor of yours in this chapter. You may even run into yourself!

41

MR. GRAB-ALL-HE-CAN-GET-FOR-HIMSELF

Erich Fromm, in his book *The Art of Loving,* states, "If an individual is able to love productively, he loves himself too; if he can love *only* others, he cannot love at all." *

Dislike yourself and you will not find it possible to like those around you.

As Fromm has also pointed out, the person who does not have an adequate self-love becomes a very selfish person. *"Selfishness and self-love, .far from being identical, are actually opposites.* The selfish person does not love himself too much but too little; in fact he hates himself. This lack of fondness and care for himself, which is only one expression of his lack of productiveness, leaves him empty and frustrated. He is necessarily unhappy and anxiously concerned to snatch from life the satisfactions which he blocks himself from attaining. He seems to care too much for himself, but actually he only makes an unsuccessful attempt to cover up and compensate for his failure to care for his real self." †

So a starving self-love leads to an aggressive self-will: "I want what I want when I want it." And self-will is the best definition of what in the Bible has been termed "sin." Indeed, it is—perhaps more than the love of money—the root of all evil.

THE KNOW-IT-ALL

That which is often termed offensive egotism is nothing more than a reflection of the lack of an inward self-assurance. This explains the mental basis of the officious person who is

* Erich Fromm, *The Art of Loving,* p. 60.
† *Ibid.,* pp. 60-61.

always certain he is right. The rigid-minded man unable to see that there may be two sides to a situation is also one who really does not love himself. The person who gets terribly upset when his viewpoint is rejected is another reflection of a lack of self-love.

NOBODY-LIKES-ME

While the lack of self-love often leads to over-aggressiveness, *it can also lead to withdrawal.* This may be observed in the person who suffers from an inferiority complex which is a lack of adequate self-confidence. Such a person withdraws from challenges, runs away from problems, bypasses opportunities, avoids moving to the center of the stage where the action is taking place. He retreats into a safe corner where his inferiority is nourished, fed and enormously strengthened in isolation. Now he can consider himself abandoned and rejected. He's convinced "nobody likes me."

Herein lies the explanation of an enormous number of cases of alcoholism and narcotics addiction. One of the reasons for the effectiveness of the Alcoholics Anonymous program is the requirement that an alcoholic stop withdrawing, retreating, running from reality, and proceed to face up to his worst self by admitting his helplessness. Only then can self-love begin to evolve.

TOUCHY TILLIE

Love yourself—or you will become hypersensitive, touchy and defensive! I recall a woman who came to me for counseling some years ago. She wanted to quit the church because she was sure people were saying derogatory things about her behind her back. I probed for concrete evidence which would substantiate her accusations. Absolutely nothing of substance could be produced. It became obvious that her views were fanciful and imaginary, verging on the paranoid. The strongest argument of the truth of her belief she could offer was, "Last week as I entered the church courtyard, three women were standing there conversing. One of them turned, looked at me and immediately started talking to the other two who began to giggle and laugh. I know they were making fun of me."

My therapeutic approach was to order her to say out loud, "I am a very wonderful person." She was stunned, flabbergasted, baffled, even unnerved.

"If you can't say, 'I am a wonderful person,'" I told her, "you must think there is something wrong with you. Tell me what it is, please."

She began to pour out her self-deprecating analysis. "I don't have a good figure, and I am not very pretty. I don't have a nice personality. And I am not a very good mother. I am not the most charming wife. I never had a college education. I am a disorganized housekeeper. My closets are a mess. I can't seem to keep the house clean. And I don't seem to be able to manage my children."

The counseling that followed helped her to see that lack of self-admiration was at the root of her problems. Spiritual therapy eventually developed within her a wonderful self-acceptance and self-confidence.

Obviously, a defensive person is his own worst enemy. Imagining that others are a threat or unappreciative will cause him to make verbal attacks against them which may turn someone who is not really an enemy into a genuine adversary.

It is obvious to any professional observer of human behavior that a major cause of human conflict is rooted in the defensive attitude of people who are unsure of themselves.

JEALOUS JACK

Love yourself—or else succumb to jealousy. Shakespeare called jealousy "the green-eyed monster." Jealousy is again an expression of insecurity on the defensive. Jealousy is a mental maneuver which takes someone else's superlative accomplishments as a judgment upon your own lesser achievements. Jealousy is a form of hating yourself for not being as successful as the person who is the object of your jealousy. You tend to tear the other person down in order to build yourself up. The person with an emotionally mature feeling of self-worth is immune to jealousy.

MRS. SMOTHER MOTHER

Love yourself—or else become overly possessive. The classic illustration of this form of self-destruction is the overly possessive mother. I recall one particularly fear-ridden woman. She projected her fears on her growing son. She imagined he might get hurt in a variety of ways. This resulted not only in over-possessiveness, but in an overly protective attitude. Since she was afraid her son might drown, he never learned to swim. He never joined the Boy Scouts; she was afraid he might get lost on a mountain trip. He was never permitted to participate in athletics; he might get injured or even be killed. Today he is a tall, broad-shouldered, muscular, two-hundred-pound baby!

Parents—love yourself or spoil your children.

45

Frequently the parent who does the spoiling is himself an emotional child in an adult body. He does not trust himself to administer the necessary discipline for fear of losing his child's affection. In other cases, the spoiling parent is unable to love himself adequately and compensates for this lack of self-affection by pouring out an extreme and faulty love upon his offspring. A three-act tragedy unfolds:

(1) He fails to love himself adequately.
(2) He fails to love his child adequately.
(3) He fails to give the child the opportunity to develop self-love.

Self-love will never develop properly in an undisciplined life. A child discovers himself through his unfulfilled wants. One middle-aged woman I knew, who was the only daughter of an extremely wealthy family, proved this to me. Her parents, who traveled widely, were constantly seeing "things" they thought their daughter might like. They lavished these gifts upon her. She told me one day, "You know, I have never *wanted* anything in my whole life. I think I have missed something of immense value by never knowing the emotion of want. My parents and then my husband always saw and secured for me all things that I could have wanted before I discovered them for myself."

HENPECKER—HENPECKED—AND SCARED CHICKEN

The overly pampered, protected and possessed child will never be able to develop self-love. He will grow up to become an extremely possessive adult. One such woman grew up as an only child sheltered by over-protective parents. She finally became a Mrs. Henpecker, extremely possessive of her husband. She became the nagging wife who emotionally emasculated her husband. Since he didn't have enough self-courage and self-confidence to face the problem, he virtually allowed her to emotionally castrate his manly qualities. He became Mr. Henpecked. They had one child—a son. That poor boy was never permitted the freedom to develop into an adventuresome young man. Grown today, he does not dare to make decisions without consulting his mother. He grew up to be Mr. Scared Chicken. This three-act tragedy ended as you might imagine. Mrs. Henpecker lives her last days in tortured loneliness. "I only got two Christmas cards this year." "Nobody ever comes to visit me." (Nobody dares! They were probably scared stiff she'd grab hold and never let go!)

THE TIGHTWAD

Love yourself—or you will never share yourself. When you receive good news you cannot keep it to yourself. You can't wait to share the good news with others. When you discover the good news that you are a wonderful person, you cannot keep from sharing it with others. You share the good news of your own wonderful self with others through a life of involvement and adventure, a life of sharing.

A man I did not know died at the age of fifty-eight, and his niece telephoned and asked me to officiate at his funeral. She handled all the necessary arrangements. I tried to arrange for a visit with her before the funeral, but she told me she was too busy. When I arrived at the funeral home, no one was there. The mortician and I waited ten minutes past the time services were to begin. Not a single person showed up.

47

It was one of the weirdest experiences of my life. The mortician mentioned that the dead man had two sons, both living in the area. Then there was the niece who had made the arrangements. This man had lived in the community for four years.

"Where are his sons? And where is his niece?" I asked the funeral director.

"The niece said she wasn't coming to the funeral herself," he replied. "And she told me the sons would not be coming. She said that her uncle never had time for them. He never had time for his community. He never wanted to be bothered by his neighbors. He never wanted to get involved in religion or politics. He was extremely selfish. He was also extremely brilliant and always managed to make money. But boy, was he a tightwad!"

He was an example of someone who never loved himself deeply enough, hopefully enough, trustingly enough, to share himself.

Love yourself—or you will drive people from you.

If you are selfish, withdrawn, defensive, overly possessive or jealous, it is certain that you will be incapable of loving other people. You prove the truism that you cannot love others unless you love yourself. You will fail in your relations with your fellowman if you fail to have good relations with yourself. Are you having problems with people? Begin to solve them by making a critical, honest appraisal of yourself.

LONELY JONESY

Love yourself—or be lonely. It is no wonder, then, that people who do not love themselves are lonely people. A lack of self-love is both the cause and the effect of much of the

48

loneliness in the hearts of people today. It puts me in mind of a man I'll call Lonely Jonesy. *He was lonely in his struggling*—for fear that people might reject him if he exposed his weakness. He was *lonely in his failure*—for fear that he might be abandoned by those who esteemed him while he was riding high. He was *lonely in his success*—for fear that friends and associates would become jealous if he shared his victories. He was *lonely in his suffering*—for fear that he might be a burden upon those he loved. (We will hate ourselves for being somebody's problem.) He was *lonely in his dreaming*—for fear that he would be ridiculed for his big thinking and big talking. (We tend to dislike ourselves when others mock us.) He was *lonely in his sinning and in his guilt*—for he feared the judgmental attitude of those whose love he needed.

When he finally came to me for counseling, I suggested that he join one of the many small sharing groups in the Garden Grove Community Church. Every participant of those groups is encouraged to "open up completely and get your troubles off your chest." Timidly at first, he started to share his anxieties. He began to share fears and joys he had never shared before. Today he's a different person. He has learned to dare to be himself and to love himself.

I'LL-NEVER-AMOUNT-TO-ANYTHING

Love yourself—or go through life achieving far less than you should achieve. Tell yourself that you are handicapped because of your race, creed or color, and you will never try to succeed. Tell yourself that people are prejudiced against you, and you will not try at all or will quit after a few feeble efforts. God knows how many people are trapped in jobs unworthy of their talents. They could be accomplishing much more if they were not slaves to their impossibility complex. "I'm not talented enough." "I don't have a good education." "I don't have enough money." So the pitiful self-deprecated image maintains its dominion over the potential greatness that waits to be liberated by a burst of self-love.

Some very sincere, well-intentioned civil rights leaders have instilled self-deprecation in the minds of the American Negro. They have gained a great following by appealing to the Negroes' lack of self-love and by declaring passionately, "People are prejudiced against you because of the color of your skin. You are the victims of racial prejudice. You are being exploited. You are being treated as a second-class citizen." Such talk is bound to strengthen the Negro's lack of self-worth. It will not build self-love which produces self-confidence which would motivate self-achievement which, in turn, builds priceless self-worth. Achievement is definitely related to one's sense of self-worth. If you think you are unintelligent, you won't attempt college. If you think you are beaten, you are. If you think you dare not, you don't. If you'd like to win but are almost certain you can't, it's almost certain you won't. Love yourself or go through life and into your grave carrying talents undiscovered, ability unrecognized.

It is amazing how many people live their lives plagued by feelings of inferiority, defeated by a lack of self-confidence, making the tragic mistake of underestimating themselves.

An unusually low estimate of yourself will result in a life of limited achievement.

Self-distrust makes quitters out of men who were born to be winners.

We sometimes see overly modest men who reduce their success potential by a false humility. Lower your self-respect, and instead of being excellent, you will be average; instead of being outstanding, you will be mediocre; instead of being top-notch, you will be second-rate.

Imagine that you are less than you are, and you will lower your self-estimation, you will lower your standards, you will abandon your dreams.

Then, priceless enthusiasm will drain out of your soul. You will go through life downgrading yourself, never striving, never achieving, until your opportunities are gone. You could sing the mournful song of the Oriental poet:

> Spring is past,
> Summer is gone,
> Winter is here,
> And my song that I was meant to sing
> Is still unsung.
> I have spent my days
> Stringing and unstringing my instrument.

LET-THE-GOVERNMENT-TAKE-CARE-OF-ME

Love yourself—or lose your freedom. If you lack self-love, you will be dominated by fear. Any individual or nation dominated by fear is destined to lose freedom.

If you fear poverty, you may surrender your personal economic freedom in exchange for security offered by a Big Brother government. The person who does not love himself lacks the self-confidence to dare to be free.

America enjoys freedom because it was founded by people who believed they were in harmony with God and could do the impossible. A strong "I can" belief will lead a young man to leave the security of his father's house and venture forth to seek his fortune.

51

It is when he believes he has potential greatness that the serf will leave the security of the fief to achieve on his own. Freedom depends for its survival on people who believe in their ability to succeed.

It was said of the ancient Jews that they made "bad slaves because they were such a proud people." Proud people refuse to allow their dignity to be stripped away through slavery. Give a man a cheap self-image of himself, and he will surrender to serfdom. Find someone enslaved by bad habits to low achievement, and give him an image of himself as a king instead of a serf—and watch as he begins to demand and then secure freedom.

This was the approach of Jesus Christ. "I am come to set at liberty those who are oppressed, to open the eyes of the blind." How did He do it? He opened the eyes of people. He told them how great they were. "You are the salt of the earth. You are the light of the world!" He said. Once they caught this redeeming self-image, they refused to remain in the chains of negative thinking. Redeeming pride will liberate you from imprisoning self-dejection and give you the freedom of self-confidence which discovers and develops your latent possibilities. When that happens, you are truly secure. For self-confidence is the only real security.

SUMMARY

LOVE YOURSELF OR DIE—PHYSICALLY AND SPIRITUALLY! Why is it that many a man dies shortly after his retirement from an active career? It may be because he has lost his sense of self-importance. He has found no compensation or substitute technique for feeding his sense of self-affection. Lack of self-love definitely affects the physical organism.

Lose your sense of self-love and you will be depressed, discouraged, lacking the enthusiasm which is the great energy-producing force of life.

Love yourself or you will die spiritually. If you do not love yourself, you cannot love your neighbor. If you do not love people, you will not be able to love God. God lives in people. If you do not love yourself and do not love people and do not love God, you are a dead man who is walking, sexing, sleeping, working, breathing, eating, excreting.

Above all else—know this: You have the freedom to form your own estimate of yourself. Be sure of this—self-estimation will determine what your self-development will be. Believe it. You can be greater than you believe you are at this moment.

I invite you to face up to the most important challenge of your life. Face up to yourself. Discover who you really are. Dare to love yourself and come alive.

IV

LOVE YOURSELF AND COME ALIVE

Discover the power of a life-changing self-image. Your life will change and the lives of others around you will change, when a power-generating self-dignity is born within you. In hundreds of cases I have seen how a worthy self-image has enabled people to conquer prejudice, overcome fatigue, lift depression, raise personal achievement levels, break destructive habits, conquer worry, fear and anxiety, generate enthusiasm, break boredom, overcome personal handicaps, change actual physical appearances and master grief and loneliness. Most importantly, when a new sense of self-worth is born within you, it can produce the emotional health that makes possible a vital and life-changing faith in a living God.

LOVE YOURSELF—AND OVERCOME PREJUDICE

The real battle against racial prejudice will ultimately be won when the American Negro comes to see himself as a wonderful person. Meet an American Negro who has a deep sense of self-appreciation, self-worth and self-esteem, and you will meet a man who dissolves white racism like ice on a summer day.

I was sitting alone in the lobby of a hotel in Torremolinos, Spain, waiting for dinner, when a handsome young Negro entered the lobby. With a wide smile exposing bright teeth and a flashing pair of eyes that radiated self-confidence, he walked quickly and enthusiastically across the lobby to face me with a winning greeting. "You must be an American; so am I. Let me introduce myself." Then he gave me his name. "It's always good to talk to a fellow citizen when you're traveling in another country."

We shook hands warmly. I had an immediate affection for this emotionally healthy person. He was vibrant, energetic, outgoing and happy. He was obviously relaxed and self-assured and very secure deep within himself. He was enjoying a life-elevating self-affection. As a result he was neither shy nor withdrawn, nor was he defensive or aggressive. He was a genuinely free and healthy personality. I was conscious of the fact that he was dark-skinned for only a brief second. The impact of his personality caused me to completely forget his race. Vibrant and radiant personalities project a spiritual force that dissolves the false impression-making impact of the physical body. We liked each other so well that we traveled together for several days.

"How did you overcome racial prejudice in America?" I asked him one day. He began to tell one of the most inspiring stories I have ever heard.

"I was born in Harlem in New York City. My father was a butcher. He told me as I was growing up, 'Son, you are a Negro. That means your skin is darker than the skin of many people. Now, my boy, there will be many people who will tell you that the color of your skin is a handicap. It need not be a drawback in your life unless you make it so. Remember this about the United States of America: it is a nation which runs on business. Businessmen are interested in making money. They hire the best men they can get at the best price. Make up your mind to be mighty good at whatever you want to be, and the profit-motivated businessman will hire you first if you are the best man available for the job. Remember something else. Everybody likes a happy person. If you are a happy person, everybody will like you. If anybody treats you badly, it's not because they hate the color of your skin. It simply means they've got a personal problem themselves. Always remember that!'

"Because this was drummed into me as a child, I was motivated to go to school, study hard and never listen to the people who tried to tell me that racial prejudice would keep me down. If I believed it, I would have become defensive and this would have only contributed to the problem. As I look back on it now, I am sure that I have encountered a good many people who were prejudiced against me because of the color of my skin. But I never allowed myself to think that way. I just went on and enjoyed living.

"I was enthused about my studies because I knew I had to make something out of myself. When I graduated from high school, I decided I wanted to enroll in a prominent business college in New York. My high school adviser told me, 'Forget it, they don't accept Negroes in that school.' I went ahead anyway and applied for admission to the college. I was not accepted. I felt they had made a mistake because I had maintained a B-plus average in high school. I boarded a subway and went up to the college. There I met a most wonderful receptionist. I told her that I had applied for admission and had been rejected. I asked if I could see the director of admissions.

"I don't know why, but she sure seemed to like me and

she said, 'Okay, just wait a minute.' Soon I was in the office of the admissions director. I liked him immediately. I said to him, 'I applied for admission here but I was turned down. There must be a mistake. I know you wouldn't want to turn me down. The reputation of your school depends upon the quality of your alumni, and I am going to be an outstanding and successful person. I'm going to be the kind of a graduate that you'd be proud to have on the rolls of your graduates!'

"He had an amazed look on his face as he said, 'Well, maybe a mistake *was* made. Send me your high school transcript with a new application.' I did. I was accepted! I was the first of many Negroes to be admitted and subsequently graduated from the school. Now I have a position as an economist with the Columbia Broadcasting System. It's a wonderful job. It has been my experience that the way to overcome racial prejudice is just to pretend that it doesn't exist. You will be a happier, more outgoing and enthusiastic person. You'll like yourself and people will love you."

LOVE YOURSELF—AND YOUR DREAMS CAN COME TRUE

A deep sense of self-worth gives rise to self-confidence. This, in turn, produces the drive that leads a person to success. After all, what is self-confidence but the belief in one's ability to succeed over difficulties? The greatest power in the world is the power of faith—in yourself, in your family and friends and in God. I am often reminded of this fact. When we were in the process of enlarging our church sanctuary, which has a long reflecting pool just outside the building running its full length, we ran into a construction problem. We would have to extend this pool. It became necessary to build a concrete bridge across the pool so that people could enter the narthex of the sanctuary. One afternoon I walked outdoors to watch the cement finisher troweling the surface of this new concrete bridge. After the usual greetings I said, "If you were asked what is the greatest power in the world, what would you say?"

I wasn't prepared for his thorough answer. Immediately he came to life. He put his trowel down, walked over to a lunch bag, opened a Coca-Cola, sat down on the grass, and looking me straight in the eye, said, "Belief!"

"You sound as if you really mean it," I said. He began to tell his story. Drops of sweat were glistening on his ebony skin. His black curly hair was salted with gray. The story he unfolded will always remain an inspiration to me. As accurately as I can recall, here's the way he told it.

"I was born one of twelve kids, the son of a cotton picker down South. My mother and father had a deep belief in Jesus Christ. The first song I remember learning was the song 'Jesus Loves Me.' My mother used to say to all of us kids, 'If Jesus loves you, you must be pretty good people.' We were told that if Jesus loved us, we could believe that He would help us to succeed.

"With this power of belief I moved to Detroit. I learned how to finish cement. My boss, who taught me the trade, said, 'Remember, this is a very important job you have. You will be putting the finishing touch on some of the most beautiful buildings in the world.' So I decided that I'd better be mighty good at it. And I was. I still am. Because I'm good at it and because I like my work, I've never been without a job. I dared to believe that I would never fail. I had five kids. I put my first son through the University of Michigan and through Wayne University Medical School. He's a medical doctor in San Francisco today! I put my second son through the University of Michigan at Ann Arbor. He's an engineer with the Cadillac company!" (And with that enthusiastic statement he was shaking his bottle of Coke high in the air.) "My third child wanted to be a dress designer. I sent her to a leading design school in New York, and she is designing beautiful dresses today. My fourth child graduates from Cerritos College this June!

"But let me tell you about my last child, my little girl. She's a beauty! When she was four years old, we visited some friends who had a piano. She came home that night and said, 'Daddy, I want to be a piano player.' And I said, 'Honey, that's wonderful! I'll buy you a piano.' I looked around for a piano and found it would cost me forty dollars a month for twenty-four months! I said to my wife, 'Let's buy it.' She said to me, 'What if you lose your job? What if you are out of work?' And I answered, 'Honey, I've always found a job. I believe I can do it.' So we bought the piano. You should have seen my little girl's eyes when they delivered that beautiful piano.

"Then I decided that I had to get the best piano teacher for her. The director of the church choir told me that the best piano teacher in Los Angeles was pretty expensive. I answered, 'My daughter deserves the best.' One afternoon on the way home from work I stopped by this teacher's house. She answered the door and I said, 'I'd like to have you teach my little girl how to play the piano.' She answered, 'Well, you see, I just don't have any vacancies.' 'I don't care,' I said, 'put my name on the list. And as soon as you can take her I'll be ready.' She looked at my old working clothes and said, 'You know, I have to charge a lot. I'm probably the most expensive piano teacher in Los Angeles.' 'Lady, look at me,' I answered, 'you can tell by my overalls and by my

60

calloused hands that I'm a working man. I work. I earn money. And I can pay the price. All my life I've been investing all my earnings in my children. I'll pay, don't worry about that.' She must have been impressed, because she said, 'I like you. I think I'll be able to take your daughter in a few weeks.'

"A month later I got a telephone call and she said, 'I just had a student move back East. If you still want your daughter to take lessons from me, I can see her Saturday at two o'clock. I took my little daughter over that Saturday and paid ten dollars for her first lesson! That was eight years ago. Last month my daughter won the trophy as the most talented piano player in her grade in the Los Angeles public school system!"

By this time he was on his feet and was spilling the Coke in his ebullient enthusiasm as he climaxed his powerful sermon to me with the words, "Reverend, the greatest power in the world is the power of belief!"

Just like this worker, if you believe in yourself, raise your sights and elevate your achievement level, you too will succeed at your chosen endeavors.

LOVE YOURSELF—AND YOU CAN HARNESS YOUR HANDICAP

As a pastor, I have known many people who have had every reason to be completely defeated by life. Crippled and handicapped in body, they somehow manage to retain their sense of personal pride which drives them to overcoming their handicaps in an inspiring way. Self-love produces soul power, and soul power generates the dynamism to shrivel mountains into molehills.

Fifteen-year-old Dorothy Perkovitch knew something was

very wrong with her when a deep mysterious fatigue first struck. Whatever it was, she hoped it would clear up fast so she could return to her lively activity as cheer leader and drum majorette in Wisconsin's Park Falls High School. But weeks stretched into months without improvement.

"I have bad news," the doctor told her Yugoslav immigrant parents. "Dorothy has been ravaged by rheumatic fever, leaving her heart in a disastrous state. I doubt if she will ever accept the elimination of physical activity. I have no hopes for her to live more than one year." Six months passed.

What was bothering Dorothy most? Was it having to drop out of high school? Was it the new pain that was now pulsating through her arms and legs? She probably couldn't say. Bravely she walked into the hospital for an examination.

"Rheumatoid arthritis," the examiners announced. Gold therapy injections, instead of relieving her arthritis, left her arms frozen at her sides and welded her immovable hip and knee joints into permanent stiffness. Six weeks later the once bounding athlete was carried out of the hospital on a stretcher completely rigid of body. This new and enormous tragedy meant that every bit of food and drink had to be put to her lips by her mother.

Dorothy now reminisces, "What I dreaded most was the inevitable day when my wonderful doctor would probably tell me that I would never recover. Yet a powerful inner voice was saying to me, 'Dorothy, you are only handicapped in body. Never allow your handicap to become mental or emotional.' "

The dreaded day came when Dorothy was seventeen. "Hey, kid, I want to talk to you," the doctor began. He was breaking the bad news. When he saw a faint smile cross her face, he interrupted his unpleasant task with, "Dorothy, I am terribly serious. You must listen. You will never walk again. You will never bend your arms or waist again."

Her beautiful black eyes sparkled as she quickly replied, "I have been listening, and I heard you very well. But, doctor, *I have brain power, I have soul power, I don't need body power!*"

Eight years passed; her body was still rigid. Still she prayed that God would at least restore her ability to write again. Then, one morning she felt a tingle in her left hand. Instinctively she tried moving her hand. Her distorted, tortured fingers began to rise slowly. Higher and higher. Now the entire arm was moving until a twisted thumb brushed the side of her cheek.

"Mom," she shouted, "bring me a dish of ice cream. I want to see if I can feed myself." For the first time in eight years, she found she could put food in her own mouth.

"Mom, bring me a paper and pencil. I want to see if I can write again." As she gripped the pencil in her twisted left hand, she thought, "I am right-handed." In her telling she says, "I forgot to tell God I was right-handed. What do I do now? It had never occurred to me to tell God which hand to reactivate. There I lay, surveying the situation, my right arm still motionless. Then, for the first time in all these turbulent years I cried uncontrollably. Through the scalding tears my eyes fell upon the crucifix on the wall in front of my bed. I looked at Him and He looked at me. As I looked, I began to listen. From deep within me I heard Him, asking —not to come into my heart—but thundering, 'Let me out! Let me find expression in you and in all that you do.'

"The distorted fingers of my left hand picked up the pen, and unhaltingly I covered the paper with words. Not only was my handwriting better than it had been, but my left hand responded more rapidly to my thoughts."

63

Driven by what she calls "deep soul power," the twenty-five-year-old girl came alive again. In five years she completed high school and rolled up high scores in extension courses from the University of Wisconsin, as she practiced her possibility thinking.

"How can I possibly earn my own way and help other people at the same time?" she wondered. The answer has come in many forms.

Today, from her bed in a city in southern California she operates a telephone answering service, runs a bookkeeping operation for small businesses and conducts courses in fashion designing, in addition to offering courses in salesmanship. It is not uncommon for her monthly earnings to hit four figures. She has purchased her own home and has a full-time housekeeper.

One day in a refreshment lounge a tall, handsome man saw her propped rigid as a fence post in a wheelchair. Something compelled him to introduce himself.

"I was thirty-one years old, and for the first time in my life, I fell madly in love," Dorothy relates. "When he started to leave after a friendly chat, I asked, 'Would you like my telephone number?'

"Before he could say anything I had written it on my napkin. It was the beginning of four years of wonderful friendship and a growing love that resulted in a beautiful wedding." Their five-year marriage is one of the happiest in the city.

"What am I most grateful for?" Dorothy asks herself. Her answer: *"It is the lack of humiliation.* I know handicapped people who suffered thirst—too ashamed to ask someone to give them a drink. I deliberately keep my distorted legs and hands exposed. I am not ashamed of them. I trust that people will come in and leave this place thanking God for the hands to open doors and the feet to walk through them. Some people tell me I can be healed. But I tell them I was healed years ago! The important thing now is that I can do something wonderful for less fortunate people with the one life I have to live. I believe God has given me a mission. And I have to carry it out."

Now, at the age of forty, Dorothy Ann Gossage has founded "Glass Mountain Inn," a development where physically handicapped people can live, learn and jointly pursue profitable business ventures. The scope of this human-dignity-restoring project is without comparison anywhere in the world. Dorothy, a great possibility thinker, explains the name of her $2 million idea this way: "It has been said that life is climbing mountains, though some people can't actually climb mountains. But anyone with soul power can make his mountain climb symbolic."

The physically handicapped person is liberated from his bondage when he discovers that he is a wonderful person —as long as he has his sanity. Discover, admire and thank God for the brain power you have; you will have a burst of new self-confidence that will help you to accomplish the impossible.

Richard D. Joy was blind, deaf and unable to speak. In order to communicate, one must be able to listen or to read the printed word. He was unable to hear the spoken word. He was unable to read the printed word. But he was taught to listen to conversation by means of his fingers. With much patience Ricky was taught to "hear" by placing his thumb lightly on the teacher's chin with his forefinger and the knuckles of his three remaining fingers resting on the throat above and below the area of the Adam's apple. Soon he began using his own vocal cords. Naturally his speech is somewhat difficult to understand when you first meet him.

But soon one grasps what he attempts to convey by voice. His next step was to learn Braille. He picked it up easily. When he became a Boy Scout he learned every one of the Tenderfoot requirements in the art of knot tying in his first lesson. He went on to achieve the highest Scout honor, elevation to the rank of Eagle Scout, and earned thirty-six merit badges! He developed into a gymnast and won awards in the San Francisco area as a wrestler. He is an exceptional swimmer, is quite at home on a pair of skis and has bowled several games better than his 162 average.

As if this wasn't enough, Ricky Joy became interested in radio and decided to earn an amateur radio operator's license. He discovered that his sensitive fingers could cover a modified loudspeaker and pick up the message. With the same technique, he monitors his outgoing signals. At the age of twenty-three he passed his FCC examination and was given license number WN6YUB. He had completely mastered the code, the theory and the technique of receiving and sending messages! As *QSR Magazine* said of him, "Let's not hear any grumbling about being too old, too young, too something-or-other. WN6YUB, Richard Joy, should be an inspiration to all of us to stop grumbling, get to work, and move ahead." It's absolutely amazing what transformations occur when a person or a people acquire a sense of self-pride.

LOVE YOURSELF—AND ENJOY A GREAT SOUL-EXPANDING EXPERIENCE

In the final analysis the greatness of a person is measured in emotional terms. You are a great person to many others if you are a cheerful, helpful, enthusiastic, optimistic soul.

I was asked to lecture to college students on the subject "Religion—A Mind-Expanding Experience." If we interpret the mind as the data-collecting section of the brain, then religion is not a mind-expanding experience. It is the purpose of education to expand the intellect. But the fact remains that the greatest intellect, a mind of cosmic proportions, can be shriveled to peanut size if the soul is restricted by negative emotions. A prominent scientist whose intellect was immense returned from an overseas trip to find his wife in bed with another man. From that moment on he was intellectually demolished by his negative emotional reaction. He admitted to me that in the classroom he found his thoughts wandering. All he could think of was his wife and that other man. A big man became a tiny man, shriveled by hatred. "My hatred was really a self-hatred," he said. "What hurt me so deeply was that I felt I had been completely disgraced, rejected, humiliated." During this period of obsession dominated by thoughts of self-debasement, he was as ineffective as an ignorant day laborer.

When he finally recovered his sense of self-love, his intellectual powers were released. He came alive again! He recovered his sense of self-dignity when he was shown that he was still a wonderful person even though he had been abused.

He learned that the value of one's self does not depend upon what people do to us—but rather upon how we react to what people do to us. He understood that he had the freedom to choose the way to react to what had happened to him. By reacting with hate, resentment and jealousy, he was literally making himself into a worthless person. By an act of will he chose to reject the negative reaction and adopt a positive attitude. He soon recovered his sense of pride. He began to develop a greater self-affection than before.

Self-love expands our soul consciousness because it clears the way for a vital contact with God. We no longer feel that we live alone and face life alone. As Kurt Lachmann wrote in a *U.S. News and World Report* editorial, "Youth is rebelling in free and wealthy Western countries and in totalitarian and poor Eastern countries. While the aims of protest differ, what could be the common denominator of motives? I can think of only one. It is the sense of forlornness in the face of overwhelming power of established modes and institutions in the mass society. It is a strictly urban crisis that has erupted in so widely diverging social systems as the United States and the Soviet Union, Germany and Poland, Italy and Czechoslovakia, Britain and Spain. It has been anticipated by the theater of the absurd and abstract art: *Forlorn men oppressed by anonymous powers and deprived of God.*"

If we are out of touch with God, we feel lonely and isolated. Something deep is lacking. It is the exciting expansion of the soul of man which is lacking.

LOVE YOURSELF—AND YOU TAP THE POWER OF THE TRINITY OF LOVE

When we love ourselves we project this radiant well-being into those around us. (Just as surely as when we dislike ourselves, we "take it out" on those with whom we come in contact.) Love yourself and you will find yourself loving the people around you. Love the people around you and you will find yourself loving God. Love God and you will find yourself conquering, with His help, the restrictive forces of negative thinking. Worry, resentment, fear, anxiety begin to leave you.

You face life with the confidence that "I can do all things through Christ who strengthens me."

You attempt great things.

You are no longer bored. You are excited with the stimulation of a chance-taking project.

You are no longer lonely. You find yourself involved with people in the pursuit of a dream.

You no longer are beleaguered by an inferiority complex.

You are discovering that you can do more than you ever thought you could do.

You are no longer sad and forlorn. You are involved in the excitement of living. Teamed up with God, living in harmony with your fellowman, you are no longer a small person with feelings of inadequacy that shrink your soul; you are tall and great, facing life and the future courageously: "With God all things are possible." "If God is for me who can be against me?"

You no longer suffer from fatigue. You are energized by a dynamic enthusiasm as the power of love for yourself, love for your fellowman and love for God surges through you.

You forget about your heartaches and your poor selfish griefs. No longer do you mournfully nurse your self-pity. You become a person with the power of God within him. Optimism, hopefulness and cheerfulness become the dominant expressions of your life.

You even have a sudden desire to break long-standing habits that have been self-destructive. You make grand and glorious resolutions. Suddenly you see yourself as too wonderful to be enslaved by bad habits. You break those habits. You have the wonderful feeling that God is helping you. Each new positive accomplishment strengthens your sense of self-worth. You feel yourself growing taller and stronger.

You rise above your circumstances. You now have the courage to make decisions and to move forward confidently after you make these decisions.

You discover that you are no longer trying to "impress people" with what an effective or successful person you are. You no longer are interested in "keeping up with the Joneses."

You no longer seek plaudits and applause—because you no longer need this external reassurance. You know that you and God are great friends. You have won God's approval. You learned to love yourself when you stood at the cross of Christ and heard the thunder of God's approval echoing from the mountain.

You discover that you are now genuinely humble. The false humility with which you dishonestly cloaked yourself was a phony impression-making maneuver. You drop it! Your hypocritical vanity is dissolved like the morning dew under the noonday sun.

You stand under the open sky beneath the love of God and simply know you are His child. Deep in your heart you know you are truly worthwhile.

You can even enjoy solitude without feeling lonely.

You discover that it's really true: when you learn to know and love yourself, you really come alive!

NOW THEN

If self-love is so personally rewarding, why don't we all naturally love ourselves?

70

V

WHY DON'T YOU LOVE YOURSELF?

Are you having trouble loving yourself? Don't be too quick to take the blame for this situation. The chances are that you are a victim of powerful sociological factors that have been slowly decaying the roots of your self-respect. Before we discover how to build self-esteem, let's look at the forces and philosophies that may be destroying your dignity, by asking some provocative questions.

I. ARE YOU TRYING TO LOVE SOMEONE YOU DON'T KNOW?

Can you love someone you don't know? Hardly. You pick up the morning paper. "Hey, Honey, there was quite a plane crash last night," you announce to your wife. "It says sixty-two people were killed." "Really? too bad," she says. "Pass the toast, dear." No tears in your cereal this morning. You don't weep for people you don't know.

71

Suppose there is a news bulletin: "Four-year-old Janet Jones fell into an open well this morning. Rescuers report hearing her cry for help." For the next thirty-six hours you hear her name, her photographed face enters your living room via TV, stories describe Janet and her family in Detroit. You begin to feel you know this child. A mounting love— and grief—begin to swell your heart and your eyes. You love her because you are getting to know her.

Do you know yourself well enough to love yourself?

MASSOPOLIS MAY BE PART OF YOUR PROBLEM

It's no secret that modern man is facing an identity crisis. It was not always so. Once upon a time Americans lived in small towns. Everybody knew everybody else's name.

How different it is in crowded, urban modern America. Few people know your name. I have used the same bank for thirteen years and am still unknown to the cashier. By the time one cashier gets to know me, she is replaced by another who demands that I identify myself when I present a check for cashing. I have to show my driver's license. She has to check the bank's file. Since few people seem to know us, we find it more difficult to know ourselves.

In the Broadway musical *Carnival* there is a winsome character who was raised as an orphan in a tiny Italian town, Mira. She ventures forth into the big world and joins the circus. One lonely night, forlorn and homesick, she walks through the darkened sawdust pathway of the tented city and sings about Mira, where everyone at least knew her name. If the many people you meet greet you with a nameless "hello" and an anonymous smile, you begin to feel more like a thing than a person: an "it" instead of an "I."

72

PLURALISM AGGRAVATES THE IDENTITY CRISIS

Once upon a time Americans were very conscious of (1) their national origin and (2) their religious faith. This helped them know themselves. To illustrate how this was, take a trip to a Swiss village. Stop in a shop and ask the proprietor who he is. He'll answer quickly, "Swiss. I am not German, I am not French, I am not Italian, I am a Swiss citizen. I am a French-speaking Swiss citizen. I am a watchmaker. I am a Catholic." His sense of identity comes naturally.

The ethnic communities in the United States—Polish, Dutch, German, Norwegian—have been disintegrating. We have become a pluralistic society. We water down our religious convictions, forget our national origins, and become as one drop in a bucket of water. If our skin is white, we lose our distinctiveness. More than we know, we have become a depersonalized socialized statistic.

WORK STYLES MAY BE AFFECTING YOU

Once upon a time the craftsman was close to his creation from start to finish. He "put himself into his work." He saw himself in the clock he built with his own hands. He was proud of his work and himself. In our highly industrialized society, the average worker is so detached from the finished product that his labor no longer mirrors himself—rather it mirrors a mass of nameless individuals.

MOBILITY CAN ROB YOU OF YOUR IDENTITY

Paul Tournier has reminded us that psychological health demands that "we have a place." Once the average person had a place to call home. It was usually the same house in the same town in which he lived all of his life. He had roots in the community. People knew him, trusted him, loved him. He knew there were those who sincerely cared about him! He knew who he was. He discovered himself in fellowship within the community. His house reminded him who he was. Doorways, windows, rooms, furniture constantly refreshed his memory, reminding him who and what he was. There were pleasant memories. "Dad always sat there." "When I was a child I played in that corner." "Mom liked to knit by that window." There were recollections which generated a sense of identity.

It is hard today to imagine families living in the same house generation after generation. If these lives were happy and healthy and the house was filled with pleasant memories, the structure itself would generate healthy and happy vibrations to those who followed thereafter. It helped create a greater sense of self-identity and self-love.

To what extent, then, does modern mobility contribute to the identity crisis? More, I assure you, than any of us realize.

II. IS THE BREAKDOWN OF THE FAMILY THE BREAKDOWN OF SELF-LOVE?

When you lose your mate through death or divorce you lose a part of yourself. Two people who live together and make love together begin to be absorbed into each other. Grief, then, is a weeping over the loss of a part of one's self that has left. Are you trying to love someone who is no longer alive?

74

DIVORCE AS A DESTRUCTIVE FORCE
FOR SELF-LOVE

When a marriage is terminated with resentment-filled divorce, torturing emotions of self-hate naturally take over. Divorced people suffer from a condemning sense of failure.

The breakdown of the family in this way is a major enemy of self-esteem. What happens to the children? "I think it's much better for our children to live in peace and quiet than to grow up in a quarrelsome home," a woman will tell me. But more often than not, this argument is not supported by the facts. The truth is that two parents who argue openly but manage to have periods of reconciliation and harmony and go on to maintain an unbroken marriage will teach their child invaluable lessons.

A child growing up in such a home will learn that you don't pick up your marbles and run away when you don't get your own way. This child will learn that problems are not something you flee from but something you face forthrightly and resolve. Such a child will enter his own marriage anticipating occasional quarrels with his mate. When this happens, he will not pack up, consider the marriage a failure, or mistakenly assume that "something has changed between us. We don't feel about each other the way we used to. I think we've lost our love. Let's call it quits." A child who has learned to expect, face and then resolve problems is well on the road to self-love.

Self-love also comes through confronting and resolving difficulties. To a mature person, every problem is an opportunity for building self-love. Every tension, trouble and trial is a challenge to move ahead with possibility thinking and triumph over the tricky trials of life.

The result? That dignified feeling that you are a wonderful, problem-facing, problem-solving person!

So much has been written about the emotional shock to the child in a broken home that it hardly seems necessary to elaborate upon it. Suffice it to say that a child is aware, at least subconsciously, that part of himself is his father and part of himself is his mother. If he detects a hostile attitude in either one of his parents to the other—and this is often unavoidable in a divorce situation—his emotional soil will be soured and will bring forth the bitter fruit of self-hostile attitudes. If he grows up with a resentful attitude toward his father, he will be inclined to project this hostility toward the fatherly qualities in his own life. Likewise, if he develops a hostility toward his mother, he will tend to project these hostile feelings upon the motherly qualities in his own life.

Inconsistent discipline produces insecurity.

Discipline tends to break down in the children of divorced parents. Every child acquires a deep sense of security through consistent discipline.

If and when the mother remarries, her name is suddenly different from that of her children. When the child, for instance, files an application card for summer camp, listing his mother as Mrs. John Jones and his own name as Billy Brown, more of an identity confusion is created in his young mind than the average parent realizes.

The maintenance of constant discipline is difficult enough in a strong family; in a broken marriage it is extremely difficult. Father has the children on a weekend. He isn't inclined to administer discipline. It's one big holiday. He comes out of the weekend a big, shining, wonderful person. Mother, who must live with the children day after day and must administer firm discipline, is failure-stricken by the rebellion of the child who refuses to accept her restraints after an overly permissive holiday with the separated father.

All of this results in a continuing breakdown of the creative forces for the development of self-love.

III. HAVE YOU SUFFERED A KNOCK FROM SPOCK?

Extreme permissiveness in contemporary society is still another self-love–sapping force. Extreme permissiveness ultimately militates against self-love. Dr. Robert E. Fitch, Professor of Christian Ethics at the Pacific School of Religion in Berkeley, California, was asked the question, "What is needed to restore health to the nation?" Part of his answer was, "There must be a change in the American home to end this long Spockian period of ultra-permissiveness. We must bring up our offspring with some sense of the moral imperatives that they will confront in life and with the sense that real authority does exist in the world."

Let us look for a moment at permissiveness and see how it relates to the development of self-love. Essentially permissiveness rises out of the desire of adults to love themselves. We feel good when we are understanding and tolerant. But over-permissiveness will cause us to dislike ourselves mildly. We begin to lose our self-respect when we allow people to "get off the hook" too easily. We may hate ourselves when we judge severely, but we also hate ourselves when we disregard the discipline of justice. Mercy and justice must somehow be balanced before we feel really good deep down inside ourselves. What human being has not mentally kicked himself on the way home from some controversial meeting, thinking, "Why didn't I say something?"

IV. DO YOU FEEL TRAPPED?

If extreme permissiveness causes problems, so does extreme restrictiveness. Man intuitively cries out to be free. Whether he realizes it or not, this insatiable compulsion for freedom has its roots in his need for self-love. Unless I am free to express myself openly and honestly, I will never know myself. Only when I know myself will I love myself. I know myself when I am conscious of talking, working, arguing or loving. Every counselor will say that many a person has found help simply by "talking out" his problems. Of course: he "sees with his ears" who he is. Theoretically, then, democracy—which encourages freedom of expression and freedom of dissent—is the political system that generates the mental and emotional climate most conducive to self-love.

But even in the so-called "free world" the individual is rapidly placed in situations where he does not feel free to express himself, lest he irritate the Establishment. Financially enslaved by his employer, he sacrifices a part of himself by restraining his aggressive feelings. The net result is that he knows himself less, respects himself less, and thus stifles his self-love.

The twentieth century could well be called the age of the highly sophisticated development of freedom-restricting institutionalism controlled by establishments. The climate has been set for the breakdown of the dialogue form of communication which encourages freedom of expression. The result? Mounting frustration which finally released itself in mass protests and rebellions—hysterical and overly dramatic attempts to communicate in an unsavory nondialogue manner with the sheltered and uninterested decision makers who run the established institutions. Our self-love is offended by the fact that we are not respected enough as persons to be able to communicate our feelings in a dialogue—the real self-love–producing form of communication.

V. HAVE YOU SETTLED FOR COUNTERFEIT SECURITY?

The peddlers of counterfeit security appealing to the fears and anxieties of insecure people add to modern man's difficulties. The alleged security that is offered by Communism, for example, is a counterfeit security. When Communism tries to spare people from competition, protect them from the possibility of failure, and shelter them from the probability of poverty, is it offering real security? Communism may be eliminating the fear of poverty and starvation, but the absence of fear is no proof of courage. What then is real security? It is a deep belief in yourself.

SELF-CONFIDENCE IS REAL SECURITY

How do we develop self-confidence? Certainly not by cowering in the herd. The individual disappears in the huge masses of people. The noted psychiatrist C. G. Jung observed this when he wrote, "Mass mindedness robs the individual of his foundation and his dignity. As a social unit he has lost his individuality and become a mere abstract number in the Bureau of Statistics. That is exactly what he is, and from this point of view it seems positively absurd to go on talking about the value of the individual. Seen from this standpoint the individual is of diminishing importance . . . the bigger the crowd the more negligible the individual becomes." *

The kind of self-confidence that generates self-worth and inner security is never born in the safety of the masses huddled within the fortress. We only acquire self-confidence when we take a chance, run the risk of failure and make good on our own. You are proud of yourself when you have faced a great challenge and succeeded.

VI. WHAT KIND OF CHILDHOOD DID YOU HAVE?

Deep-rooted unfortunate childhood experiences are often the cause of a later lack of self-love. For that reason, careful analysis by a competent psychologist will often reveal reasons from our childhood why we have hung up our self-love in a lonely and long-forgotten closet of our memory.

We now recognize that a child who has felt rejected by a father or mother is bound to develop self-love problems. We are all familiar with the problems of the child who is overly loved in childhood. Consider the typical child movie star. Such famous children find themselves pampered, adored and spoiled. When they reach adulthood and may no longer be the center of attention, they develop real problems. They are unable to love themselves without extravagant adulation and pampering.

Consider the child of the famous father or mother. Almost inevitably he will be tempted to compare his own achievements with those of his famous parent. If his self-love is based upon personal achievement alone, he is bound to have great difficulty loving himself unless, by one of those rare

* C. G. Jung, *The Undiscovered Self*, p. 16.

exceptions, he should surpass his highly successful parent. More often than not he grows up underrating himself. He develops a pitiful self-image, eventually retreating into obscurity or rebelling to gain attention or resenting the world for not accepting him as it does his parents. In a variety of self-destructive ways he moves through life suffering from a lack of self-acceptance, self-esteem and self-worth.

It is easy to see how a child reared in poverty could develop too low an estimate of himself. A successful man, fifty years old, well dressed and outwardly confident, still imagined himself an unworthy person. During counseling he recalled some incidents from his poverty-stricken childhood. His family lived just within a school district which included the richest people in the city. He had to wear old overalls to school while the other children were dressed in the finest clothes. Telling about his boyhood, he poured out story after story of abuse, ridicule and embarrassment. A sad self-image sprouted in adolescence and still dominated him. He thought he had successfully buried these self-humiliating childhood memories. As I pointed out to him, "You can bury a tin can. It will rust. You can bury a piece of wood. It will turn to dust. You can bury an old bone. But you cannot bury a worm." And childhood rebuffs are like worms. They will rise again and again, often in distorted forms of aggression, neurotic ambition, or other negative personality traits.

VII. IS MONEY ROBBING YOU?

Oddly enough, affluence as well as poverty can sometimes deprive us of self-esteem–generating experiences we might otherwise have.

On a camping trip some years ago, I faced what appeared to be a minor crisis in our family. We were miles from home when it was discovered that my small boy had forgotten to bring his toys. My limited budget left no money to buy my son the sailboat he wanted. We decided to build one. The whole family spent an adventuresome day collecting sticks, scraps of cloth and nails. With a hunting knife we carved the hull from scrap lumber. From a discarded handkerchief we made a sail. The mast was a willow stick. The keel was a tin can flattened out and nailed firmly to the bottom of the little craft. The building of this toy became an exciting family project! It was an unforgettable thrill as the children watched this toy take shape. "Do you think it will really sail, Daddy?" Bobby asked doubtfully. "Of course, Bobby," Sheila rebuked him. Then, with the unshakable confidence of a six-year-old child, she added, "Everything Daddy makes always works." Bobby's eyes sparkled with newly revived faith in the whole project. "Hurry up, Daddy, let's try it," he urged. We jammed the mast in the hull, pinned the sail in place with a safety pin and headed off for the lake.

There was an appropriate christening ceremony on the shore. We named her "Queen of the Lake." After spending some hectic minutes convincing my youngest that he could not ride on board, we launched her! The sail trembled as fearfully as a child about to take his first step, then, as if gaining sudden confidence, the sail billowed forth, pulling with increasing speed the new Queen across the water on her maiden voyage. "She sails! She sails! She sails!" the children cheered. In that moment I felt rather proud of myself. A lack of money to buy a sailboat opened the way to a great self-exhilarating experience. My somewhat impoverished state gave me a sense of self-esteem which the financial ability to purchase a sleek, perfectly produced boat in a toy store never could have done.

VIII. DO YOU FEEL LIKE AN ELEPHANT-DODGING ANT?

The threat of nuclear destruction certainly works against man's self-love. He finds himself a quivering ant, dodging the thundering feet of thermonuclear elephants. Thus far we have avoided this fate, but we cannot help considering ourselves potentially helpless at the threatening feet of this overpowering monster.

Likewise, the age of automation and computerization degenerates man's dignity. To the extent that it diminishes the creative power of man and depersonalizes the human being (at the same time conjuring up an image of an all-powerful electronic machine that keeps a constant eye on us), it contributes more than we understand to self-disturbing tension.

IX. HAD A MEDICAL CHECKUP LATELY?

I remember how a friend who was enthusiastic, self-confident and outgoing demonstrated all the qualities of an individual who had achieved a mature sense of self-importance. Then, without apparent cause, he developed a growing depression and with it a loss of self-affection. This in turn produced irritability and related personality difficulties. I advised him to have a physical checkup. He returned, saying that the doctor had discovered he had diabetes! In still another case out of my counseling files a psychiatrist discovered a thyroid deficiency. Are you losing your self-esteem? Maybe you should see your doctor. It might be physical.

X. WHAT KIND OF SELF-IMAGE DO YOU HAVE?
or
HAS MODERN ART SMEARED YOUR SELF-PORTRAIT?

Extreme realism in modern art is yet another development which contributes to man's loss of self-reverence. Sculpture reached its most glorious peak in the golden age of Greece when the human form was shaped in a most idealistic—yet representational—style. Then, art was designed to inspire man with an ennobling self-image—exalted and idealized. Art began to deteriorate in Greece when the male figure was depicted in a more feminine way.

In earlier American culture, art forms in sculpture, literature and painting tended to portray the ideal person. Ignoble persons were either redeemed or condemned. Art was considered great art when it inspired man with a noble self-image.

A reaction was inevitable. In reality no person is perfect. Our present philosophy screams, "Tell it like it is. Art must be an expression of what man is, not what we wish he was." As a result, on the stage and printed page we often see ugly portraits of mankind. The result? Depicting man at his worst leaves us with a fairly ugly self-image. What happens? Inspiration to greatness? Hardly.

When art passes a negative judgment on mankind, leaving us in the merciless mud without inspiration to redemption, then art is an obscene sacrilege profaning man's self-reverence. Art, then, becomes immoral.

What is immorality? Anthing that deteriorates human dignity or assaults man's inherent self-worth!

XI. BEEN HOODWINKED WITH DARWINIAN MONKEYSHINES?

Santayana once said, "As sure as somebody gets a good idea somebody else will come along and carry it too far." This has happened with the theories of Charles Darwin. Never in human history, prior to the twentieth century, has man believed that he may be nothing more than a glorified monkey. The contributions of Darwin are recognized. Regrettably, his theories and conclusions have been carried too far by some philosophical speculators. *The process of evolution has been turned into a philosophy of evolution by materialists who grasp for a system which can explain man without God.* For ages upon ages, man looked upon himself as a unique creation of God. What this did for man's sense of self-reverence is incalculable. Now we have anthropologists like Desmond Morris who tell us that we are nothing more than naked apes. Mr. Morris spends nearly 100,000 words probing this concept. When Mr. Morris concludes, as he does in the final chapter of his book, that man is destined to become extinct as a species, we have been given the full self-love–annihilating treatment.

XII. BURNED WITH SPARKS FROM MARX?

The teachings of Karl Marx are still another phenomenon undermining human dignity. Never before in the history of human civilization has there been such a finely tuned philosophy that contends that man is an intelligent computer made of bones, flesh and blood which functions best on sex and steak. *In Marxism, man's value is measured by his*

85

productivity. He is a tool—not a person. What a blow to self-love. Two American Communists were discussing the case of Kathy Fiscus, a young girl who fell in a well several years ago. A total of $250,000 was spent in an attempt to rescue her. Unfortunately she died before she could be rescued. One Marxist commented, "How ridiculous to spend a quarter of a million dollars. She could be replaced in nine months' time with a more brilliant child. We could mate a more brilliant father and mother with the odds being the production of a superior female. The quarter-million dollars could have been used to build a hospital!"

Lenin was wrong when he predicted Communism would be the "wave of the future." I boldly predict that Communism will ultimately fail, for it fails man's ultimate will! It violates human dignity and militates against man's need to love himself.

XIII. HAS RELIGION RUINED YOUR FAITH?

Religion, too, has long been guilty of robbing man of a healthy self-love. Not a single existing religion has clean hands at this point. Hinduism has its caste system, Buddhism has a denial of the self and Christianity has its unique problems which I shall discuss in more detail.

Orthodox Christianity made its first mistake when it failed to distinguish between self-love and self-will. A person is made to feel guilty whenever he has a wonderful feeling of self-importance. The result? He represses those ennobling sensations of self-love that come through honest achievement, genuine self-discipline and self-sharing. He does not dare to enjoy these healthy emotions for fear of being condemned as vain and proud.

How did Christianity get so warped? Actually it began with Aristotle three hundred years before Christ. The Greek philosopher recognized man's almost instinctive inclination toward self-recrimination. Holding a twig in his hand and bending it backward, Aristotle illustrated how the human being tends to bend backward: condemning, belittling, criticizing, running himself down. Aristotle's solution, as he bent the twig forward, was to advise man to push forward. We have to puff ourselves up, strut and swagger and say, "What a great guy I am!" Out of this Grecian philosophical posture there evolved a sort of person who was haughty, pushy, puffed up, boastful. The result? A dangerous and distorted arrogance that found great delight in looking down condescendingly on all who were on a lower social level. Against this background Christianity appeared with its doctrine of "humility."

A great problem arose when an attempt was made to translate the Christian concept of self-regard into Latin (the first language in which the philosophy of Christianity was put into concrete form). A Latin scholar has said, "There is no word in Latin which adequately expresses the sense of self-esteem which as Christians we ought to have." The Latin translators, reacting against Aristotle's concept of puffed-up pride, took the teachings of St. Paul and used the Latin word *humilitas* in trying to describe what we ought to think about ourselves. Unfortunately the word *humilitas* was more descriptive of the idea of downgrading yourself, running yourself into the ground, saying "I am no good," with the inherent suggestion that if you ever think of yourself as a wonderful person and have a normal sense of self-love, you are being sinful.

In contrast, Christ always tried to give man's self-image a

87

boost. When He met immoral people He never called them sinners. Never! "Follow me and *I will make you* into wonderful people," He said. One of the most despised members of His society was the Jew who was a tax-collecting tool of the Roman army of occupation. Such a man was Zaccheus. When Jesus met him, He might have judged him harshly. Instead, He sought to build this man's sense of self-love by offering to spend the night at this two-faced tax collector's house.

It is interesting that the only persons ever accused of being horrible sinners by Christ were the very narrow-minded, legalistic, hyperreligious people. "A generation of vipers," He called them. What did they do that was so hellish? *Under the guise of authoritarian religion, they destroyed man's sense of self-affection and self-worth.* Perhaps nothing destroys one's sense of self-respect more than the finger-pointing, wrist-slapping, fist-shaking religious authority which claims to speak in the name of God.

Dr. Samuel Shoemaker, a prominent American churchman, said, "Religion can never be the answer to human problems. All of the religions of the world are inadequate. Christ alone is the answer. Christ alone understands. Christ alone forgives. Christ alone eliminates your guilt. Christ alone saves and then assures you that you are God's child and the most wonderful person possible! Christ alone fills the human heart with love—joy—peace—self-confidence. No wonder a genuine Christian really loves himself."

This—more than any other social, economic, psychological or political reason mentioned or unmentioned in this chapter —is the real reason we don't love ourselves adequately.

We have lost touch with Him.

VI

START WITH A CLEAN SLATE

My wife and I took the hydroplane from Naples to the Isle of Capri. What an experience! Along with many other tourists and residents, we filled the large boat to capacity. While moored to the dock, it seemed almost to be sinking in the bay. Slowly it surged forward, gradually picking up power like a giant jet airplane until, skimming along on four skis, it virtually flew over the water. We were hydroplaning past heavy tugs that chugged their way sluggishly through the sea.

What a parable of human life! We are weighted down with all sorts of mental burdens, as we plow along like sluggish tugs trying to push the whole weight of the ocean ahead of us. We should be rising above it with power. Human beings were designed by God to hydroplane through life, skimming over the rough waves, flying high, traveling smoothly and rapidly.

That's exactly what happens when we achieve self-love.

Nothing drags our self-love down more than depressing guilt. What is guilt? How does it destroy your self-love? How can we wilt our guilt and disclaim our shame?

GUILT IS A PARTICULARLY HUMAN PHENOMENON

Dr. Viktor Frankl has pointed out that "no other animal experiences guilt." The Austrian psychiatrist explains, "The dog who runs under the table after he has wet the rug is not experiencing a guilty conscience. His response is merely a conditioned reflex. The dog merely anticipates punishment which he customarily receives after such behavior."

Authentic guilt is the negative emotion experienced by a "conscience-mind" that passes a personal moral judgment upon itself. This phenomenon is known only to Homo sapiens. Immanuel Kant observed, "Two things astound me— the starry heavens above and the moral law beneath."

GUILT IS ENORMOUSLY WIDESPREAD

THE RICH feel guilty when they drive through the ghetto, which explains why some millionaires turn against the system that has produced their wealth.

THE POOR, comparing themselves to the wealthy, condemn themselves as failures. Joshua Liebman observed, "Guilt is the accusing sense of failure."

SAD AND SICK PEOPLE feel guilty when they suspect they are a burden on family and friends.

ACTIVE AND SUCCESSFUL PEOPLE find themselves feeling guilty at play. "I really should not be here. I have so much work to do."

DIVORCED PEOPLE suffer from easily understood guilt. WIDOWS are also guilt-prone. "Having fun?" I asked an American widow in Istanbul. "Not really," she answered honestly. Knowing I was a pastor, she confided: "Ever since I lost my husband four years ago I feel guilty every time I start enjoying myself. Here I am spending the money he worked so hard to save."

UNPOPULAR PEOPLE feel guilty: "I must be doing something wrong or I would have more friends."

POPULAR PEOPLE have their own variety of guilt. "I've been so busy I haven't had time to return his call—I completely forgot her birthday." "I have so many friends that I can't keep in touch with them all and it bothers me," a friend confessed to me the other day.

THE UNDER-ACHIEVER has his turn with a disturbing conscience: "I know I should be doing better."

THE SUCCESSFUL PERSON discovers that he too is not immune to guilt. "I'm so busy being successful that I don't give enough time to my family and my community."

ADVANCED AGE brings no assurance of final freedom from guilt. Old people still battle their accusing conscience: "Why didn't I?" and "Why did I ever?" questions arise from a lifelong collection of regrets. "I feel I'm a burden on my children." "I'm so useless I feel guilty for living."

GUILT IS THE GREAT IMPOSTOR

Our will to self-love generates a determined resistance to recognizing our own guilt. The result? Guilt takes deceptive forms—sometimes extreme generosity or religiosity. More often, in our effort to protect our self-esteem from the assaults of guilt, we rationalize our feelings only to find ourselves suffering from neurotic, negative emotions. True self-love helps us understand the forms our guilt takes.

WHAT'S YOUR PROBLEM?

HOW OFTEN THE COUNSELOR ASKS THAT QUESTION.
HOW SELDOM WE HEAR AN HONEST ANSWER.

"I'M FEARFUL"

Are you sure it's fear? Perhaps your real problem is guilt masked as fear. What, after all, is guilt?

1. Guilt is fear of exposure. "What if they find out the truth about me?"

2. Fear of exposure is really a fear of judgment. "They'll call me on the carpet."

3. Fear of judgment is really fear of rejection. "They'll fire me if they find out!"

4. Fear of rejection is actually fear of humiliation. "I'll be so ashamed if anybody finds out."

5. Fear of humiliation is really fear of the loss of self-love. "I'll hate myself if this ever gets out."

The fear of death is the mother of all fears. Why? Deep within man there lurks an instinctive expectation of ultimate justice. Man cannot believe that evil men can get so neatly off the hook simply by dying. For example, the thought that Adolf Hitler has escaped justice in eternal sleep or nothingness is repugnant to human dignity. I don't believe I have ever preached a sermon on hell, and yet I find people without any religious background coming to me expecting ultimate judgment upon their souls for their sins. Until this guilt-rooted concept is eradicated, they will never know freedom from fear.

Fear of death is not only the fear of judgment, but a deep-rooted fear of the possible extermination of self. The will to self-love cries out for survival of the self. This explains the universal belief of most religions in some form of an existence beyond death. People who love themselves love life and never want it to end. Meanwhile, the guilty long for nothingness. Nihilism, which believes in nothingness, is a neurosis, then—a sophisticated philosophy to satisfy the death wish of the non-self-loving person.

"I LACK FAITH—IN MYSELF—IN PEOPLE— IN GOD"

Perhaps your real problem is guilt hiding behind doubt. The guilty person, who is worried about judgment, defensively attempts to discredit "the judge." I know a man who was snobbish though brilliant, an intellectual agnostic. He blissfully assumed that his unbelief was the product of extreme intelligence. When, during a period of stress, he underwent psychiatric analysis, he recalled a childhood fight with his mother. He remembered going to Sunday school, where he was told, "God will send you to hell if you hate your parents." At that moment his tender young mind "emotionally turned God off." From that moment his conscious mind began to fabricate an elaborate philosophy of atheism. When he came to see that his unbelief was rooted in the negative emotion of guilt (fear of a judgmental God), he took a free and fresh look at religion. Today he is a dynamic believer in a loving God.

Doubt is the defense mechanism of a guilty person trying

to clean his conscience by eliminating the source of moral judgment. Guilt is a major cause of religious unbelief. More than any of us realize, it explains the motivation behind secularism and the God-abolishing mood of our day. We seek a neurotic escape from judgment simply by discrediting the judge. When this guilt-induced "let's-discredit-the-judge" thinking takes place within ourselves, it leads to a loss of self-love. My worst self, fearing judgment from my best self, discredits the best self. "I don't believe I'm a wonderful person." So a wounded self-love, seeking to save itself, actually destroys itself. The result? "I don't believe in myself."

Since there can be no love without faith, it follows, as night follows day, that

> IF YOU CANNOT TRUST YOURSELF
> YOU WILL NOT LOVE YOURSELF

Moreover, we can easily see how a guilty person will not trust others. We tend to project our faults on others. The adulterous husband suspects his wife of infidelity. If you want to discover a person's secret temptations or sins, notice what he accuses others of doing. He will give himself away! Only guilty people are capable of suspicion. The innocent are incapable of distrust. It explains why childlike faith is so sincere.

"I'M LONELY"

Analyze yourself—you may discover that loneliness is really guilt in masquerade.

What is loneliness? What's the difference between loneliness and solitude? Loneliness is emptiness within yourself—solitude is inner fulfillment. Inner fulfillment is the fruit of happy talk, sweet communion and rich fellowship with our self, our friends or our God.

Look at the way the guilty person deprives himself of the emotional fulfillment that comes through fellowship: Fearful of exposure to life, he withdraws from people, who then leave him alone in his insecure isolation. What happens now? Does he enjoy rich fellowship with himself? Hardly. Left alone with his self-condemning mentality, he begins to agonize in loneliness, (1) remembering his past mistakes, (2) recalling his sins of omission and commission, (3) imagining what's going to happen to him in the future. He quickly becomes bored—or lonely.

By contrast, a self-respecting person welcomes isolation as an opportunity to have fellowship with himself. He recalls his accomplishments, relives the happy moments stored in his memory and hopefully reflects on his optimistic future. The result? He strengthens his self-love in solitude.

> Time to a self-loving soul is solitude.
> Time to a self-condemning soul is loneliness.

Guilty individuals, incapable of enjoying constructive companionship with themselves, suffer loneliness. Self-loving persons, capable of creative communion with themselves, enjoy solitude.

"I'M LOVE-STARVED"

It follows that guilty people are love-starved people.

Guilty people DO NOT love. Guilt is a condemning conscience. What's that? Your best self is passing judgment upon your worst self, sentencing your self-esteem to hell.

95

That, certainly, is not an exercise in loving, for loving is not condemning but forgiving.

Guilty people DARE NOT love. To love is to reveal your soul. This is a risk guilty people dare not take. He who feels guilty never dares share his deep feelings. He dares make body contact but dares not make contact eyeball to eyeball. He may draw close to people physically but remains aloof emotionally. The result? Lonely in the crowd, bored at the party, spent but unsatisfied in the love nest.

Guilty people CANNOT love. Since the heart of love is trust, there can be no affection where there is no confidence. Can you trust your jewels to the care of a thief? Because the guilty mind is self-condemning, it does not trust itself enough to love. "I'll probably bungle this situation, too" is the thought. Because this type is self-distracting, he considers himself too unworthy to give or take love.

The love-starved, guilty person considers himself too empty of self-love to give love, too unworthy of self-love to accept love.

"I BATTLE HOSTILE FEELINGS"

Sally sat in my study and poured out her bitter feelings. "I feel angry toward the whole world." "Have you ever really done anything to make you feel guilty?" I asked. She broke down and admitted she had been unfaithful to her husband. This guilt made her defensive; she felt like a cornered rat. She became, as I described above, a guilty, love-starved person. Love-starved people become angry people. After she confessed and accepted forgiveness, her hostility was dissolved in a rebirth of self-worth.

"I CAN'T GET OVER MY GRIEF"

Marilyn wept as she said this, two years after I buried her husband. I remembered how active she was in club activities before her husband's death, how tall and strong she appeared prior to and during the funeral. I recalled that intimate moment in the chapel after all the mourners had left—save for this woman and her pastor. In that unguarded moment she threw herself over the cold corpse and cried, "Oh, my darling, I'm so sorry for the nights I left you alone —for the cross words I spoke to you—forgive me, please," and she broke into uncontrollable sobbing. Now, two years later, she was still condemning herself.

"My friend," I counseled, "have you forgiven yourself?" "What do you mean?" she queried. I reminded her of her confession over the casket. "Did I say that?" she asked. "There's always been guilt mixed in with grief," I suggested, adding, "but you're deliberately nursing your grief in a desperate attempt to atone for your guilt. This is understandable—but ridiculous. This is nothing more than destructive self-flagellation. Stop condemning yourself and stop hating yourself. Start forgiving yourself and start loving yourself—come alive again!" Prayer therapy did the trick. Her guilt gone, she became a happy, active worker in her community again.

HOW YOU CAN ERADICATE GUILT AND "HYDROPLANE" THROUGH LIFE

1. **Remember You Are Human.** Don't be ashamed of your imperfections. Discover your humanity. "To err is human—to forgive divine." If you experience guilt, you can be positive you are a normal human being.

2. Analyze Your Guilt. Begin with this question: Am I really guilty? You may not be as guilty as you think.

I know people who are going through life unnecessarily feeling guilty because an authority figure imposed it on them. The authority figure is only projecting his own personal sense of guilt upon others—a most irresponsible, negative emotional reaction. We've seen it happen in religion for years: a minister will accuse others of the shortcomings he sees in his own life.

Diagnose your guilt feelings. *You may not be as bad as you think you are.*

UNCOVER YOUR SUBCONSCIOUS GUILT

You may be suffering from actual guilt without realizing it. The mind has enormous capacities for rationalization and repression. We use these powers to stifle our conscience when it threatens our self-love. How does this work? By rejecting the moral authority that would provoke a guilty conscience. We defrock the judge on the bench. We tell ourselves the Ten Commandments are outdated. We tell ourselves we're clean, but underneath we suffer from anxiety, nameless fears, mysterious tension or frenetic fun-seeking. *You can chloroform the conscience but you cannot anesthetize the subconscious.*

SEEK PROFESSIONAL HELP

A professional counselor, sensitive pastor or qualified psychiatrist can help you to discover if guilt is the cause of your lack of self-love.

EXPERIENCE FORGIVES

Reassurance is not enough. You must experience redemption from all guilt. Discover the peace of mind that comes through an experience of forgiveness.

FORGIVENESS IS DIVINE

Nature does not forgive. If you cut your hand off, no matter how much you may weep and repent, the hand will not grow back.

Society does not forgive. It keeps records. When we move from one job to the next, our new employer checks our character and efficiency with our previous employer.

Computers don't forgive. They record facts and retain them.

Educators do not forgive. Do poorly in school, and at the end of a semester, no matter how much you may repent or beg forgiveness, you will be graded according to your record.

Religion does not forgive. It tends to point the finger, slap the wrist or shake the fist.

Psychiatrists *cannot* forgive. A psychiatrist said in one of my classes: "Only psychiatrists can remove guilt from human lives, for only psychiatrists really forgive. Our ethical standards require that we remain morally, ideologically and religiously uncommitted. We pass no moral judgments; we remain morally neutral. We are not bound to a judgment standard; we will not be judgmental. The patient knows this and consequently dares to unburden himself freely to us."

This psychiatrist made one grievous error: A person who is not committed to a moral, spiritual or ideological standard of judgment *cannot forgive*. If he is uncommitted, he has not been offended.

ONLY THE OFFENDED CAN FORGIVE

HOW TO EXPERIENCE FORGIVENESS

1. *Reveal yourself* to a wonderful person who is deeply committed to all that is beautiful in life.

2. *Risk rejection* as you openly confess your guilt to him.

3. *Experience acceptance.* Shocked, you will discover that instead of shaming you, he accepts you.

4. *Encounter real love in action.* Now you will be experiencing real love—a rare experience. Most love that we experience is a calculating, counterfeit affection. People love us if we agree with them; if we think, talk and act the way they think we should; if our friendship is helpful to their ambitions. Real love is unconditional, uncalculating, nonselective and nonjudgmental.

5. *Start loving people this way.* Experiencing unconditional love will make you feel so great that you'll start loving people in the same unconditional, nonjudgmental way.

6. *Expect people to accept you.* We tend to expect people to treat us the same way we treat others. Criticize and condemn people and you'll be suspicious—you will then expect people to criticize and condemn you too. The reverse is equally true. If you love everyone with an unconditional love, you'll believe they love you in the same way. Your guilt will suddenly disappear! No longer are you fearful of exposure, condemnation and judgment!

Try to find that wonderful person from whom you can experience and learn nonjudgmental love.

HERE'S THE PERSON WHO CAN HELP YOU

He is the famous Jew from Nazareth—Jesus Christ. He came into the world preaching and teaching a religion called the Gospel, which means "good news." What is the good news? The good news is that we can be completely forgiven and really respect ourselves again.

The life and death of Christ were spent demonstrating real nonjudgmental love. Even as He was dying on the cross, He prayed: "Father, forgive them, for they know not what they do." It was a dramatic moment in history when Christ proved that God can forgive any sin. Who *really* forgives? Society does not. Nature does not. Education does not. Religion does not. Psychiatrists *cannot*. Christ *can* and *does* forgive.

Why does God want to forgive us? Because in forgiving us He helps us to love ourselves. And only when we love ourselves will we dare to believe that we can and will become the sons of God that we were created to be.

Do you still have a problem with guilt? There's a part of you that is mercy-seeking—craving forgiveness. There's also a part of you that is demanding that you pay the penalty. That is not necessary. Repeat this prayer and you will achieve the forgiveness you crave.

Jesus Christ, I accept You as my forgiving Savior. I don't understand what Your death on the cross means. But I know that in some way You died for me. I remember the old Jewish prophet who spoke about You when he said, "He was wounded for our transgressions, he was bruised with our iniquities, the chastisement of our sins was upon his shoulders." I remember an Indian chief who once said, "Fire cannot burn where fire has already burned." You have by Your suffering and death on the cross accepted the responsibility of my sins. You have fulfilled the justice that demands that wrong be punished. And You mercifully promise to extend this forgiving credit to my account. By Your death justice and mercy are both fiulfilled. Thank You, Jesus Christ. Amen.

Now go out and love people the way God loves you and you'll start loving yourself.

VII

TEN TIPS TO LIFT YOUR SPIRITS

Are you ready to go to work and try to reinforce your struggling self-love?

Here, then, are ten tested spirit-lifting tips that could lead you to a new life. I've tested them with hundreds of people and they work. Now let's look at these techniques and see how effective they really can be. They can work wonders—if used properly.

I. JOIN A STATUS-BUILDING CLUB THAT COMMANDS RESPECT IN THE COMMUNITY

CASE HISTORY: I knew him for years as a shy man with a strong inferiority complex. He was insecure, withdrawn, introverted. One of his few close friends talked him into joining a downtown service club. In this fraternity he finally found himself. He felt genuinely accepted by people he'd always looked up to. For the first time in his life he began to believe that he was likable. The transformation was remarkable. Today he is outgoing, enthusiastic and chairman of a committee to raise money for the club's favorite charity!

CASE HISTORY: Jane Doe was unkempt, backward, awkward, tense. Born into a poor family, married to a common laborer, living in an untidy home, she was a classic illustration of a nobody-likes-me person. Her neighbor, Mary Smith, was active in Garden Grove Community Church—head of a department that was responsible for recruiting volunteer labor in cleaning up rooms. One day Mary was desperate for help and called Jane. "Could you possibly give me a hand tonight in my church?" Jane didn't know how to say no. Four hours later she found herself in the company of four strange women who were the friendliest people she had met in her whole life. "If you ever need help again, let me know," she offered enthusiastically as Mary drove her home.

What has happened since is a beautiful story. She became a regular volunteer. Leaders in the church talked to her often and sincerely complimented her wonderful work. She made a great discovery. She was appreciated by respectable people. Today she is a church member and has the esteem-boosting joy of knowing she is "in" with a wonderful group of people. Now her house is clean; her hairdo and dress style are simple but neat and attractive. Everybody says, "Isn't Jane wonderful?"

EVALUATION

We discover ourselves in involvement with others. Fellowship with people is a mirror whose reflection shows us who we are. It is difficult, if not impossible, to love ourselves until we are accepted by people we esteem. *Be daring*. Push yourself forward and join at least one noteworthy club or organization in your community. *Do remember:* You'll get no more out of your membership than you put into it.

CAUTION: Don't make the mistake of thinking you are somebody just because you're "in." That is the danger of club-joining—membership itself doesn't necessarily mean you are automatically acceptable. If you become a snob, your phony ego will inflate without reason, and your self-respect will go on the skids.

II. TACKLE A CREATIVE PROJECT

Creativity of all sorts builds self-worth. When one woman I know feels depressed, she bakes a pie. A fellow minister lifts his spirit by tending to his garden. Another housewife refinishes her old furniture.

CASE HISTORY: George was a high-school dropout who was drafted into the Army as a private and assigned the job of cleaning latrines. This further depressed his self-respect. With his "I don't-give-a-damn" attitude he finally got into real trouble. He was given a week in the stockade for disobeying an order.

"What are you going to do when you get out of the Army?" the chaplain asked him one day after he completed his sentence. "I don't know, Chaplain." "Why don't you go back to school? You could finish high school while you're still in the Army, then go to college when you get out. The G.I. Bill will help pay for it." "Me go to college? I'm not smart enough," George answered. "I think you are! Try taking one course and I'll help you," the Chaplain said. "Let's see if you're not smarter than you think. God put more brains in your head than you realize."

He tried. He started with that one course, moved on, and by the time his hitch was up had a high-school diploma. He was accepted by Hope College, my own alma mater. He was a rightly proud young man when he got his sheepskin. Today he holds the rank of commander in the United States Navy.

EVALUATION

A high-school diploma, a certificate of accomplishment, an academic degree, can work wonders in building self-esteem. It is possible to prove to yourself that you can become skilled—or that you are intelligent.

PRESCRIPTION: Check the trade schools if you are a practical-minded person, or the local colleges and high schools. You'll find people much older than you in the classroom. Enroll in the next class. Start slowly. Move ahead. And wind up discovering the greatness that was waiting to be developed within you.

WARNING: Achievement alone is not necessarily an assurance of self-worth. We all know highly educated people who are unbearably egotistical. Their academic accomplishments have gone to their heads. They look down on their colleagues who graduated from institutions lower on the academic status pole. They snub the noneducated as "low achievers" and "nobodies." We know others—truck drivers and laborers—who are among some of the most appealing, steadfast people on the face of the earth. *Remember:* In the final analysis, greatness depends more on the development of character than on professional accomplishment.

INSIGHT: The man who is always displaying his credentials to impress people still has a long way to go.

106

III. BUY NEW CLOTHES

Don't you feel like a new person when you put on some new clothes? My wife recently bought a dress for an older woman, a shut-in member of my congregation. She tried it on and wow!—what a change in her self-image. She felt young and pretty again.

A young high-school dropout, bearded and long-haired, shabbily dressed, was offered a job as an automobile salesman with the stipulations that he get his hair cut, have a shave and show up for work in slacks, white shirt, tie and sport coat. He did; after all, he was hungry for some cash.

"You never saw such a change in his personality," his mother reported a week later. "He talks, walks and acts like a young prince."

When my four-year-old daughter is dressed in her play slacks she is a lively terror at home. Dress her up in a new lacy dress for Sunday school, and she fairly tiptoes in a ladylike way through the house.

The first time I visited a young hospital patient, she was depressed. The second time around she was in high spirits. Her hair had just been styled, she was wearing a beautiful new gown, and her nails had been manicured. The effect on her spirit was amazing.

Famed showman Florenz Ziegfeld once ordered diamond necklaces at a cost of $250,000 to be worn by his showgirls. "How ridiculous," a colleague argued. "Use rhinestones, no one will know the difference." Ziegfeld snapped back, "The girls will know the difference."

Morris West, in *The Devil's Advocate,* describes a character who gave his self-esteem a lift every day simply by buy-

107

ing a fresh carnation and putting it in his lapel. He immediately walked a little taller.

I borrowed a friend's new Cadillac the other day. Driving down a street of shining store windows, I saw myself in that beautiful car mirrored in the windows. I was really impressed. I looked and felt like a big shot!

EVALUATION

Does this illustrate a way to build self-worth? Yes—and no. Yes—if a new suit of clothes, car, hairstyle, gives you a renewed self-image strong enough to inspire you to become a finer human being. Yes—if it gives you a respite from self-hate. But be careful. These are only props that tend to make you a better performer—not a better person. *Warning:* Clothes, cars, cosmetics will do more harm than good to your self-respect if you use them primarily to make a big impression. If you carefully selected these stage props to mask the real YOU long enough to "make a hit" with someone—then you're on shaky ground! New anxieties may arise —fear of exposure, concern that your real self may be uncovered. You may even begin to dislike yourself as a cheap actor.

CONCLUSION: Give yourself a treat. Get something new and pretty. Enjoy yourself. But remember: Corsages fade quickly, hair styles don't last long, clothes wrinkle quickly and new cars lose their glamour terribly fast. *Resolve:* to find stronger supports to a genuine self-love.

IV. PICK A CHALLENGE AND GO AFTER IT

Find out what you're made of. Prove to yourself that you've got some good stuff in you. Many a human being with an inferiority complex has been motivated to high achievement in an effort to prove himself to the world. As a result, he is able to direct his life into an extraordinary series of accomplishments. He may become a prominent doctor, a top-flight engineer, a benevolent missionary or a thoughtful statesman. Many people benefit from the drive which motivated him. He experiences real self-worth. From conquest to conquest, from mountain peak to mountain peak, from one challenge to the next, he moves through life proving to himself that he is worthy.

"WAR AMPUTEES SKI WAY TO CONFIDENCE" is a headline in the newspaper today. The story:

> "If a man loses a leg in battle, all the card playing, television watching and good dinners in the world won't rehabilitate him," says James E. Johnson, director of the California Veterans Affairs Department.
>
> His prescription: "Make him use his remaining leg, and the artificial one, when it is fitted, as soon as possible."
>
> One specific cure prescribed by Johnson is a ski trip on mountain slopes that "few persons with whole bodies will attempt."
>
> Just before Christmas such a trip was planned and arranged by Johnson for 17 amputee Army veterans of the Vietnam fighting.
>
> They were patients at Letterman General Hospital in San Francisco, where they had been outfitted with artificial limbs and had taken their first faltering steps in a rehabilitation program.
>
> The men were bussed to a weekend of skiing at Beacon Hill Lodge, Soda Springs, between Sacramento and Lake Tahoe.
>
> There they were met by members of the National Amputee Skiers Association—Bill Rablin, president; Wilbur Earheart, who also is a member of the National Ski Patrol; Jim Graham and Dan McPherson.

They are amputees, too, and they soon showed each veteran how to put his best and only foot forward in learning the basic steps on maintaining balance, how to walk, turn and tumble on skis.

And tumble they did.

But before the day was over the veterans had mastered the gentle slopes.

They thawed out at the lodge that night and hit the higher slopes the next day.

Those precarious slopes were faced as bravely as had been the Viet Cong bullets, land mines and booby traps which had taken the veterans' lower limbs only a few months before.

Two doctors from Letterman hospital watched the vets turn from tumblers to fairly accomplished skiers. They were Majors Pat Carolan and Boris Stojic. Said amputee Pat Carolan, "This [skiing] is unsurpassed for restoring a man's confidence and determining his degree of mobility."

EVALUATION

PRESCRIPTION: Try something you've always wanted to do—but never thought you could.

CAUTION: Don't kick yourself down if you don't succeed. Pat yourself on the back as a good sport who had the nerve to try. *Remember:* You can accomplish great feats and still be a flop in the business of being a great person. On the other hand, you can fail in every conquest and still be a lovable soul. Nothing is more important than that!

WARNING: Make certain the challenges are creative and uplifting. We all know neurotic characters who turn into promiscuous playboys or flirtatious females in their self-destroying attempts to build self-love in the game of challenge and conquest.

V. BECOME A GOOD RECEIVER

This is one of the problems of the person who doesn't love himself. He doesn't know how to receive. We have learned that "it is more blessed to give than to receive." But it's blessed to receive too. We grow in self-esteem when we learn how to accept suggestions, constructive criticism and sincere compliments.

You will come to like yourself when you see yourself improving. How will you ever become a better person if you consistently, instinctively, impulsively defend yourself against constructive criticism, refusing to see the wisdom of suggestions from friend and sometimes from foe? Welcome, listen, analyze, evaluate and apply the positive aspects of criticisms and suggestions.

Learn to accept compliments. We all need them. Who does not require periodic reassurance? You'll be dishonest with yourself and dishonor yourself if you immodestly (and dishonestly) reject genuine praise when it comes your way. I know one man who is a great guy, but he doesn't know it or believe it. As a result he is timid, tired and tense. Basically he is kind, considerate, and creative. Strangely enough, he doesn't see himself as the man he really is.

He always backs away from compliments. "Oh no, that's nothing—I'm not doing very much" is his typical reaction to well-earned praise. "You're a lousy liar," I finally said to him. "It's high time you start telling the truth. Next time I compliment you, I want you to tell the truth. Humbly but honestly admit the fact that you have tried hard and, thanks to many others, you're happy you've done a good job. You can't give out what you won't take in. Accept compliments

111

and you'll start handing them out. The result? You'll begin to enjoy real self-esteem."

EVALUATION

ADVICE: Accept compliments—they can help you. But don't seek them out. Let service be its own reward.

WARNING: Compliment people honestly but never insincerely or you will hate yourself for the phony you are. Moreover, such flattery will only harm the recipient. He will be encouraged to seek the narcotic of recognition only to suffer tragic withdrawal symptoms when the fix is not forthcoming.

REMINDER: If you know you can receive real praise, you won't have to fish for compliments.

VI. GET TO KNOW IMPORTANT PEOPLE

It will do wonders for your self-respect if you earn the friendship of an important person. Is there someone to whom you look up with awe and admiration? Tell him so. Make his personal acquaintance. Write him a letter. Telephone him. You'll be surprised at how approachable he is.

EVALUATION

Do try it without fear of rejection.

WARNINGS: Don't become a name-dropper. Don't try to "use" the person. He'll drop you if you're only trying to "use your connections." Imagine what will happen to your self-esteem if he drops you cold.

REMINDER: The most important person you can know as a personal friend is Jesus Christ. He really makes you feel worthwhile. Prayer, of course, is the way we communicate with Him.

VII. CLIMB THE LADDER

Strive to rise to a higher position in life. Why not? You'll prove that you've got more on the ball than you thought. You promote your self-respect when you are promoted to a higher position. Through honest labor and sincere dedication, you can rise higher on the social or economic scale than you are now.

EVALUATION

Go to town! Set some higher goals for yourself.

WARNING: You will need something beyond position to keep your self-love alive. One day you'll have to retire. If professional position is the first and foremost foundation of your self-esteem, what will you do when some young fellow starts coming up the ladder after you? You can run into real problems here.

If you have to scheme, manipulate and politic your way up, you will not prove anything to yourself or anyone. You'll only be demonstrating that you are a clever manipulator, a shrewd politician, a smart operator and a heel.

President Woodrow Wilson related how one of his maids approached him the day after the Secretary of Labor had just resigned from the Cabinet. "Mr. Wilson," she said, "my husband is a laboring man. He knows what labor is. He understands laboring people. I would like to request that you consider appointing him as the new Secretary of Labor."

To which Mr. Wilson replied, "Well, you must remember, the Secretary of Labor is an important position that requires a big man." The maid replied, "But if you made my husband the Secretary of Labor, he *would* be a big man!"

REMINDER: The position does not make the man: the man makes the position.

VIII. STAND UP STRAIGHT AND TALL

It is understood that the mind controls the body. Think of yourself as inferior, and your shoulders will drop. Imagine yourself as upstanding and you will stand erect. It is also true that the body can affect the mind. Stand as straight and tall as you can and walk this way. You will find yourself feeling more self-confident as a result.

I once counseled a man we'll call Paul, who could only feel tall when he had a couple of martinis. "Nothing builds my self-confidence like a couple of drinks," he told me.

The cocktail hour has achieved enormous acceptance because it enables people to narcotically elevate their spirits, partially obliterating the collection of self-disgracing experiences of the day. Unfortunately, the euphoria of a cocktail withers about as quickly as the bloom on a rose.

"You're in danger of becoming an alcoholic," I warned Paul. "When alcohol is consumed to satisfy emotional needs —watch out!" "Next time you feel the need for a drink," I advised, simply take a deep breath, stand as tall as you can. Feel how high you are. Feel your body growing taller. Lift your shoulders. Raise your head as high as you can." It wasn't easy but it worked: Paul has given up drinking as an emotional crutch.

114

EVALUATION

Physical well-being will contribute enormously to spiritual well-being. The physical being can affect the emotional response. Build self-esteem by improving your physical appearance. Are you overweight? Diet and exercise will help improve your figure. It'll pay great dividends. The pride of having a trim figure is far more satisfying than the brief pleasure of fattening food.

LIMITATIONS: A beautiful body does not automatically insure a beautiful personality. Real self-esteem will come with emotional fulfillment more than from physical attractiveness.

WARNING: Watch out for the body cult—it can produce more narcissism than genuine self-esteem.

IX. BE A CONSTRUCTIVE NONCONFORMIST

"Be not conformed to the world but be transformed by the renewing of your mind" (Rom. 12:1). This is very wise advice to take. Our natural inclination is to use conformity as another mechanism for manipulating ourselves into a state of strong self-acceptance.

We make the assumption incorrectly that social acceptance will result in personal acceptance. Fearful of rejection by those around us, we tend to conform, in the belief that this will lead to popularity. A popular person stands out from the crowd. He is distinctive, an inspiring leader of the group. The conformist is often lost in the shuffling of the masses. He never experiences the pride of leadership that comes to those who dare to be different. The conformist never discovers himself as an individual; he only knows himself as a member of the group. When you dare to be distinctive, you realize you are an individual. When you conform and become another insignificant part of the whole, you feel more like an object. Conformity leaves you with an "it" complex. Inspiring nonconformity leaves you with an "I" consciousness.

This does not mean that we are to become revolutionary, antisocial, rebellious nonconformists. Extreme negative reactions will only stimulate negative emotions—anger, hate, cynicism. You won't love yourself if you're filled with negative emotions!

Negative nonconformity, marked by rebellion and destructive criticism, destroys self-respect. Nonconformity should be positive, creative, constructive and inspiring. *Positive* nonconformity, distinguished by creativity and a respect for others, results in self-esteem.

Look at the case of Mabel.* "I did everything wrong from the day I started work some years ago in the gear factory. First, I was given a uniform which consisted of a shirt and a pair of slacks. Strange as it may sound, I had never worn slacks before. So I didn't know whether the shirt should be worn inside or outside the slacks. I decided outside.

"No sooner had I started to follow a man named Danny to my work table than I realized my decision was wrong. All the other girls looked very trim with their shirts tucked neatly inside their slacks, and dainty kerchiefs peeping out from the pockets of their shirts. I heard giggles as I walked by with my flapping shirttails.

"We finally arrived at a long bench where twenty men and women were at work. I was given an instrument called

* *Guideposts* Magazine, June 1968.

116

an air gun. 'Look it over and get the feel of it,' Danny told me.

"When Danny turned on the air, the gun began to jump like a bucking bronco and I screamed. Some at the table were amused; others just looked scornful. Danny calmed my fears and then gave me an old gear to work with. 'In time you'll learn to grind these to a radius of one thousandth of an inch,' he said.

"I didn't really believe him and I was ready to quit. Having recently lost both my husband and my father, I was very lonely and unsure of myself. Furthermore, I had lived a sheltered life and was quite naïve.

"After several weeks of struggle, I did learn to grind the gear to one thousandth of an inch. My self-confidence began to increase.

"But by now I had another problem. I could tell that I was not accepted by the 'gang' in our department. They were not rude or hostile—just, well, aloof. I tried to be a part of the women's group as they gossiped in the powder room, but I always seemed to say the wrong thing.

"One night, Art, who worked just across from me, came around the end of the bench and gave me a long sheet of paper with one end folded over. 'This is a chain letter to Walt,' he explained. Walt had been inducted into the Army only a month before.

"Not knowing Walt, I started to hand the letter to the girl next to me. But Art would not accept this. 'You can write something. Look back over what's been written and you'll get some ideas,' he insisted. I did so and discovered that almost every letter contained words to this effect, 'When the gang gets together I'll hoist a drink for you.' Not being a drinker, I still did not know what to say.

"My mother had taught me since childhood to pray about every situation I faced. She would even pray about a cake she put into the oven. So I bowed my head and some lines of verse came into my mind. I picked up my pencil and wrote down words like this to the unknown Walt:

> I, too, will drink for you,
> In a church beside a table
> Where a group has knelt to pray.
> And the drink will be
> A special kind of brew.
> The time will be Communion
> And we'll drink the precious wine.
> As we drink we'll say a prayer
> That God will shield you and
> Your pals from danger.
> So remember that we care,
> As you fight on some foreign field.

"I folded the paper and gave it to the girl next to me. Then suddenly I realized that my words would be read by everyone else down the line. Sure enough, as the next girl passed the paper on, she pointed to the verse I had written. Now I really set myself apart, I thought. My depression grew until I was sure that I just did not belong here.

"The next day I was at my bench when I saw Danny heading for me. Here it comes now, I said to myself. I'm about to be fired. Danny came behind me and said, 'Mabel, please shut off your gun.'

"I turned to look at him, and his eyes were gentle. 'Mabel,' he said, 'we in the office read what you wrote to Walt and we want you to know how proud we are to have you in our factory.'

"For the rest of the day I was in a kind of daze. Everyone

seemed so friendly. 'Mabel, will you write a few lines for me to send to my boyfriend overseas?' . . . 'Mabel, will you write a verse for me to give my parents who are celebrating their thirtieth wedding anniversary?'

"Though this experience happened some years ago, I've never forgotten the truth I learned from it. Winning acceptance and esteem from other people comes not by compromising one's principles, but because one remains true to himself and God."

EVALUATION

Self-esteem can be nourished when you know you are respected by your associates. You will respect yourself, even if rejected by your community, if you are true to your own convictions. Be a constructive, kind and creative nonconformist, and hostility will turn to admiration.

WARNING: Don't fall into the trap of becoming negative, critical, cutting, condemnatory or judgmental, or you'll become a self-righteous, holier-than-thou troublemaker.

X. OPEN UP OR BLOW UP

CASE HISTORY: On the outside Bill appeared to be pleasant and agreeable. On the inside his ulcerated stomach was bleeding. As I came to know Bill well, I discovered that he was actually churning inside with angry and frustrating emotions. He bottled up these feelings until they turned into poisonous sores. He was, of course, trying to love himself by gaining the respect of people and by avoiding conflict. Okay—but he was going about it in a destructive way! He was helped to understand this fact of life: When we turn

119

our aggressive feelings inward we do not avoid conflict—we only shift the battle scene to the lonely arena of our mind.

Once I received a traffic citation for traveling 45 miles per hour in a 35-mile zone. I am embarrassed when I think how I allowed this to upset me. My respect for the badge and the law-enforcement authority restrained me from saying anything then. However, as I drove on down the road with the insulting ticket, I found myself battling the police officer in the arena of my mind.

"You are terribly unfair," I said to him as he sat on his motorcycle in the right-hand corner of my cerebellum. "Don't you realize, officer, that I was on this section of road for only a quarter of a mile and there is no speed limit posted in that section of the highway? How was I to know it was a 35-mile zone and not a 45-mile zone?" From the haunting mirror of my memory, he glowered back at me. I struck out at him again in my imaginary bout.

This continued for ten minutes until I realized that I was trying to build up my offended self-esteem through mental conflict. How ridiculous! I was missing the joyous view of the mountains to the right of the road and the orange grove-bedecked valley to the left. I was lost in my own world of frustrating conflict—a futile and absolutely hopeless way of trying to rescue my sinking self-love. I tried to forget it but I couldn't. I had to open up or blow up.

How does one handle this kind of situation? Open up positively instead of negatively to resolve conflicts. Once more I faced the uniformed patrolman in my mind and said, "You know, you men have a tough job. You have to enforce the speed limits. Obviously, you can't put a posted sign every quarter of a mile on every highway. The truth is you were trying to protect me from accident and injury. I was wrong.

120

You were right. I don't mind paying the ticket. It will be a donation to the local library, or perhaps the school system will benefit in a small way from the fine." As soon as I began thinking this way, I realized that I was truly building moral self-esteem!

EVALUATION

Conflicts are inevitable—and a major cause of self-hate. Face them negatively and all hell will break loose. You may gain temporary relief, but you'll hate yourself in the long run if this approach becomes a behavior pattern. To shut up and say nothing can be almost as dangerous.

To repress, ignore and reject conflicting emotions or ideas destroys one's self-concept. When this happens to a man in a marriage, he loses his selfhood, de-sexes himself emotionally. We come to know him as a spineless, henpecked husband. When this happens to the wife she never builds the self-confidence that comes through self-expression. She evolves into a totally dependent female absolutely incapable of facing life alone, if circumstances such as widowhood make it necessary.

SOLUTION: Look upon every conflict as an opportunity. Here's your chance to show how big you are. Open up. To speak your mind in a frank and friendly manner will be helpful. Then think and talk about the positive qualities in the situation and build upon them. You'll love yourself when you know you're wise enough, big enough, to see both sides of a conflict.

Review the ten tips to lift your spirits. Read the list which follows and select those which can become most meaningful to you.

1. Join a status-building club that commands respect in your community.
2. Tackle a creative project.
3. Buy some new clothes.
4. Pick a challenge and go after it.
5. Become a good receiver.
6. Get to know some important person.
7. Become a climber.
8. Stand up straight and tall.
9. Be a constructive nonconformist.
10. Open up—or blow up.

SUMMARY

You are on your way to acquiring a healthy self-esteem when you have lifted your spirits. Move ahead now and discover ten steps to a strong self-love.

VIII

TEN STEPS TO A STRONG SELF-LOVE

You can give your self-esteem a boost—and you should—by following the ten tips given in the previous chapter. The real key to self-love, however, lies in self-discovery, self-development, self-discipline and self-dedication. It is through these processes that you can become a genuinely great human being. Here, then, are ten concrete steps which will help make you the person you want to be, the person you should be.

I. GET RID OF YOUR FEAR OF FAILURE

This is the very first step in building a strong self-love. Let us again consider why we don't love ourselves.

1. We don't love ourselves because we don't know ourselves. "You can't love someone you don't know." We are unaware of the remarkable potentialities which are within us.

2. We don't know ourselves because we are afraid to find out what kind of person we really are.

3. We are afraid to face up and honestly meet ourselves for fear we might discover we are failures, and we are afraid of failure!

Why are we afraid of failure? We fearfully believe that our friends will forsake us if we fail. We're afraid we will lose all self-respect if that should happen. In trying to spare our self-love from the wounds of humiliation, we actually surrender to the dominating fear of failure. We deliberately allow the fear of failure to restrain us from plunging into what might be a humiliating experience. *The fear of failure, then, is a self-contrived defense mechanism subconsciously fabricated to shelter our insecure self-love from possible embarrassment.*

It's a cinch you will never love yourself until you get rid of the neurotic fear of failure.

SEVEN STEPS TO ELIMINATE YOUR FEAR OF FAILURE

1. Realize that you are not really afraid of failure; understand that you are actually afraid of losing your self-esteem. Here is the way the thinking process operates:

If I fail I will be rejected by those I love.
If I lose my friends I will be humiliated and ashamed.
If I'm ashamed I'll hate myself.
Therefore I must protect my self-love by yielding to a fear of failure.

2. You must come to understand that this fear of failure,

rather than protecting your self-love, actually chokes your self-love. However, you will not love yourself if you are dominated by a fear of failure. Rather, you will tend to become jealous, or hypocritical, or perfectionistic, or selfish, or aggressive, or resentful. If you turn into that kind of a negative emotional person, you will surely hate yourself.

3. Realize that cowardice is more shameful than failure. It is no sin to miss the mark. It is a self-disgracing, self-dishonoring experience to give in to fear and not even strive to succeed. I conquered the fear of failure when I read this sentence—"I'd rather attempt to do something great and fail, than attempt to do nothing and succeed."

4. Understand that good people never abandon the courageous, honest, enterprising loser. They will understand, sympathize and give you the strength to begin over again. They will abandon you only if you abandon yourself.

5. Learn this important lesson: People accept or reject you not for what you *do,* but for what you are. We all know some successful people who are rejected because they are mean, crabby or deceitful, while we know others who have not achieved as much and are surrounded by people who love them.

6. Eliminate perfectionism. Think realistically: Nobody is perfect! No intelligent person really expects anyone to be perfect. People will not reject you (and you will not reject yourself) when you admit imperfection. People will reject you and you will reject yourself if you go on living a lie by pretending to be perfect.

7. Remember, if you do fail, admit it and start over again. All the world loves an honest and truly repentant person. In the entire roster of great human beings listed in the Holy Bible, only one man is called "a man after God's own heart."

That man was David. Strangely enough, he committed the sins of murder and adultery. But he knew how to repent for his failures openly, honestly and sincerely. Psalm 51 has these revealing lines: "A broken and contrite heart, O God, thou will not despise." Good people never abandon someone who admits he failed and honestly wants to begin over again. In fact, genuine friends will come to his side and try to help him start over again.

II. DISCOVER THAT UNIQUE PERSON CALLED "YOU"

When you have conquered your fear of failure, you'll dare to discover that remarkably different individual called YOU. How do you discover yourself? We have already seen some answers in this book. To summarize:

You discover who you are:

(1) In adventure. Here you discover your hidden potential.

(2) In freedom to stand on your own feet. You may succeed or fail, but at least you'll find out what you're made of.

(3) In belonging—to a family or a group.

(4) In fellowship. Deeply sharing your fears and hopes with people you can trust.

(5) In involvement. Getting active in causes you believe in deeply.

(6) In creativity. Whether it is a book, a song, a pie, a garden or a painting.

(7) In responsibility. Shun responsibility and you will never discover your capabilities.

(8) In self-discipline. Here you discover your hidden power.

BE YOURSELF AND DISCOVER YOURSELF

Sam is fifty-six years old. All his life he has—sometimes mildly, sometimes severely—hated himself. Why? Listen as he sits in my study and pours out his story. "All my life I've tried to be somebody else. I never dared to be me. I didn't think I was good enough. So I've been a phony for over half a century. That's the trouble with people—they're all trying to be somebody else, and that's impossible!"

REVEAL YOURSELF TO DISCOVER YOURSELF

If you want to love yourself, you have to know yourself. You'll never know yourself until you *are* yourself.

You'll never really discover yourself until you strip away the false fronts you have been wearing. Only then will you discover the real YOU.

We strive desperately to keep our real self a secret even from ourselves. The possibility of self-disclosure is frightening to most people. We do all kinds of things to cover up. Clothes, cars, cosmetics are frequently masks that we put on to try to kid ourselves and others. Be honest enough to dare to allow your real self to be unveiled. Stop hiding behind fear of exposure, fear of rejection or a fear of seeing a failing personality. Don't ignore the opportunity to know yourself well enough to improve yourself.

You can muster this honesty by understanding that no one is perfect and that nobody expects us to be perfect. Erase perfectionism and you will dare to be honest.

127

Tell yourself: "I am in need of improvement. We all are. And I will never learn to love myself until I know my strong points and my weak points."

DO THIS

1. Find a trustworthy friend who knows you well. Tell him, "I want to be honest with myself. Help me. What are my strengths and what are my weaknesses?"

2. Honestly and openly share yourself (as you see yourself) with this friend. It's amazing how you will come to see yourself in a new light if you will drop all barriers, remove all fears, relax deeply and simply talk your problems out in the presence of a sensitive and sincere listener. We discover ourselves when we listen to ourselves talk honestly and openly. We see this in counseling sessions all the time. A man or woman with a problem sits down and, feeling confident and secure in the presence of a professional, pours out his or her troubles. The therapist sits silently with friendly eyes and folded hands, in meaningful spiritual rapport, and listens with an understanding and sympathetic ear. When the troubled person completes the tale of anguish and prepares to leave he often says, "Thank you so much for what you have done."

How did we help? Just by listening with a caring ear which encourages the opening up of mind and heart. The troubled one discovers himself—his weakness and his strength —in the process of creative conversation, even if we contribute few actual words.

3. *Listen* with an honest ear to your friends' sincere compliments and constructive criticism. Remember we often hear with a prejudiced or preoccupied ear. You will be a better

listener if you say, "Tell me the truth. Lay it on the line. Hold nothing back. Let me have it straight. I'm ready to find out the truth about myself."

A PREDICTION

If you are honest in talking and listening, here is what will happen:

1. You'll feel vastly relieved. You'll be proud of yourself for daring to share yourself honestly.
2. You'll discover that you weren't as bad as you thought.
3. You'll discover that you have positive qualities you weren't aware of.
4. You'll also discover that some of your shortcomings which you thought were minor are far more important than you've admitted to yourself.

III. COMPLIMENT YOURSELF

Now that you are honest with yourself, start complimenting yourself. You have heard your strong points. Probably you won't really believe them until you hear yourself spell them out. So start talking—out loud. "I am a kind person." "I am a good worker." Mention all of the admirable qualities you've just heard about.

DEHYPNOTIZE YOURSELF

As you compliment yourself you will begin the slow process of dehypnotization. For many years you have hypnotized yourself into believing the worst. You have been saying (and believing): "I'm inferior. I'm not attractive. I'm not very intelligent, charming or talented." Now you can break this negative spell that has gripped you for years. You start dehypnotizing yourself when you start complimenting yourself. It's not easy. You'll feel boastful, vain and hypocritical—but you've got to do it!

You're like a piece of furniture covered with layer upon layer of ancient paint. Peel, scrape and wash off the layers of camouflaging enamel and discover the rare woods underneath! From childhood on you have been covering your real self under layers upon layers of self-criticism. You can peel off those layers of self-condemnation and expose a great heart deep down inside! That's what happens when you dehypnotize yourself by complimenting yourself.

IV. FORGIVE YOURSELF

This is the last stage of a self-refinishing process. While the old paint may be stripped off, there still remain the stains of self-condemnation, regret and remorse which must be eliminated. You may have conquered your guilt to the point where you realize that God has forgiven you, but you probably still are not forgiving yourself. You still recall and ponder some of the mistakes of your past.

Although it may be difficult to keep self-despising memories from coming to mind, you don't have to give them a hearty welcome! Don't invite them in for a visit! Slam the door in their faces. God has forgiven you. Forgive yourself. When you bury the hatchet, bury it deep. Don't leave the handle above the ground. Simply affirm, "Christ lives within me—so I am a wonderful person. Christ has forgiven me.

I have forgiven myself." Keep repeating these affirmations, and find yourself forgiving yourself.

Now give yourself a pat on the back. Stand up straight and tall. Face the sun. Smile and once more repeat the affirmations aloud. It may be necessary to find a lonely spot in the remote countryside where you can shout these affirmations as loud as possible. Actually shout them out! For the subconscious mind is sometimes only reached through enormous vocal volume.

V. IMPROVE YOURSELF

When you compliment yourself you are beginning to improve your self-image by offsetting the negative qualities you may have.

Begin by believing that you can improve. Build confidence by reminders that you are constantly changing.

> YOU ARE NOT THE SAME PERSON TODAY
> THAT YOU WERE YESTERDAY

This poses an important question. Can you love something or someone that is constantly changing? Can you trust something or someone that is in a state of flux? Remember, you cannot love that which you do not trust. It is almost impossible to love the impermanent *unless it appears that the changes are for the better.* We regard with interest and anticipation an antique, or a growth stock. A person who is *growing* intellectually, or spiritually, will also be so regarded.

How, then, can we also love our changing selves? *By*

131

realizing we have the power to choose if we will change for the better or for the worse.

You can change your physical self. You can control the shape of your figure by exercise. If you are fat, you can diet and become slim. If you have a gloomy face, with drooping skin, sleepy eyes and hollow cheeks, you can change this to a large degree by an improved attitude. The face will quickly alter its contours, its shape and its projected mood by responding to the attitudes of the mind even as the ocean responds to the wind that blows over it. Just as the ocean presents a constantly changing scene—sometimes calm, sometimes rippling gaily, sometimes crashing with white fury over jagged rocks. Your face is a sea that will change according to the winds of emotion and thought.

Don't fear change. Welcome it as an opportunity! If change is a great problem, it is also a grand human hope. One word, one illustration, one idea can transform the whole complexion and the destiny of our life. I see this happening constantly. Some positive idea falls unexpectedly on the mind and changes forever the destiny of an entire family. Thank God we are not created to be rigid, nonchanging objects of marble, granite or steel!

As a pastor, I am often called in times of tragedy. Invariably I find myself giving those who are grief-stricken this advice: "You cannot change what has happened. Accept that as fact. Accept another fact: This tragedy will either make you better or worse. It will draw you closer to God or it will drive you away from God. It depends on how you choose to react to your tragic situation."

You cannot always control what happens in life, but you can control your reaction to the event. Look upon every experience, whether good or bad, whether a triumph or a tragedy, as a challenge to make you a better person. You will then begin to see yourself as a "positively compulsive improver." You will trust and love yourself.

VI. ACCEPT YOURSELF

You've complimented yourself. You've forgiven yourself. You're learning to improve. Now get ready to accept yourself.

There are certain aspects of your being that are unchangeable. You will never change your heritage or the color of your skin. A Negro militant confessed, "I was really fighting 'Whitey' because I was in fact hating myself for being black. I resented my color and my circumstances, so I hated all white people whose pale complexion reminded me constantly that I was dark-skinned. They reminded me of what I wanted to be but never could. I can see now how my resentful unwillingness to accept my color was a stupid attitude. It only led to more anger, hate and violent thoughts. Whites, I now realize, were not my real enemy. I was my own worst enemy. Since then I have changed my attitude. I accept with pride the color of my skin. I find I am a different person. I am relaxed. I carry no chip on my shoulder. It's amazing what a wonderful relationship I have with whites now."

Remember, if you allow yourself to become disgusted or upset about your unchangeable physical appearance, it will definitely affect the expression of your face. The reverse is also true. You have probably seen people who did not appear attractive on first acquaintance. But because they had such a wholesome self-love, they were outgoing, enthusiastic and cheerful. After getting to know them, you thought that they were truly handsome or beautiful.

Accept yourself. God made you the way you are because

133

He wanted you to be distinctive! He likes what He created. You should too.

VII. COMMIT YOURSELF TO A GREAT CAUSE

Commit yourself to a cause worth living for. Get out of the grandstands and onto the playing fields. Move into the spotlight of creative and constructive involvement. It is the risk-running racer on the track, not the hotdog-eating grandstander who gets the attention, the applause, the encouragement and, finally, the prize. Because the chance-taker is in the spotlight, he attracts support and succeeds. And he wakes up one morning with the really big prize—self-confidence. Remember what has been said earlier—self-love is gained through adventure. Attach yourself to something bigger than yourself. In involvement you will acquire a sense of belonging. By a commitment to people, projects or causes, you will have an opportunity to assume responsibilities. *Responsibility generates self-love, for responsibility fulfills the need to be needed.*

Be willing to be used by a cause, a project or a person with a great dream. But if you commit yourself in the ambition to become important, you may do your self-esteem more harm than good.

VIII. BELIEVE IN SUCCESS

It is vital that you develop a strong belief in your ability to succeed. Whether you are committed to a group project or a private project, you must, you can and you will succeed.

Develop a technique for success.

How do you do this? First, DREAM. Get a problem-

134

solving, human need–filling idea. If you don't have a dream, how can it come true? In the process of dreaming something magnificent, self-love will come alive within you. Dare to plunge into your dreams. Dr. John Schindler, in *How to Live 365 Days Out of the Year,* tells us that we should always be planning something. Dr. William Marston, an outstanding psychologist, said at the Madrid Conference on Psychiatry, "I've noticed that successful people have two qualities: thoughtful work, and they are positively impulsive." Build a dream for yourself if you want to succeed.

First you need a dream, and then you will need a SCHEME. Develop a schematic blueprint—a plan which includes several realistic ways in which you could conceivably fulfill your dream. Be a possibility thinker. Nothing is impossible to the possibility thinker.

A TEAM is the next need. No man is big enough to make a big dream come true if he's working alone. You can accomplish the impossible if you recruit the intelligence to advise you and work with and for you.

Now build a BEAM under your dreams. Support your dream with faith, hope, and prayer. This will keep you from quitting during the difficult times that almost always occur. Now put a GLEAM on your dream. Dedicate your success to the service of God and to your fellowmen. Put a soul in your goal. Selfish success generates self-will; generous success builds self-esteem. Surround your dream with the trinity of faith, hope, and love.

> Faith stimulates success.
> Hope sustains success.
> Love sanctifies success.

135

IX. STRIVE FOR EXCELLENCE

In all of your striving for success, strive also for excellence. Do the best, whatever you do. You'll love yourself when you know your achievement is of high caliber. Everyone can excel in some area. Perhaps you can become the most thoughtful person in your community—the person who never forgets to send a get-well card or a thank-you note.

Strive to excel in generosity, and you'll enjoy living with yourself even more. The generous are also enthusiastic, warm and self-loving. Tightwads are tense, suspicious, hesitant, worried souls who have never tasted the joy of self-love.

X. BUILD SELF-LOVE IN OTHERS

This is the last step to building a strong self-love. Forget yourself now, and start thinking of people around you who think too poorly of themselves. You can give their discouraged, depressed spirits a lift, and in so doing find even more reason to regard yourself as a person of worth. When that happens, you will know you are a truly worthy person.

IX

HOW TO BUILD SELF-WORTH IN THOSE AROUND YOU

He was a handsome Negro youngster. I guessed his age at about twelve years. "Shine, mister?" he asked. Certainly he was one of the most ambitious shoe shiners in New York City, for it was past eight o'clock on a Saturday night when I climbed onto the well-worn seat built on the back of his stand. Without delay he dipped his slender brown fingers into the can of black wax and began smearing the scuffed toes of my oxfords.

"What's your name, son?" I asked. He looked up with two handsome dark eyes that sparkled with life and vitality. He kept slapping polish on my shoes as he answered, "Jimmy Wilson, sir!"

"That's a great name, Wilson," I told him. "We once had a President of the United States by that name."

That made a real impression on him. For a moment he stopped work. Then he seemed to shift psychological gears, as he transformed himself into another personality. He dropped the well-stained shining cloth, letting it hang limp over my left shoe. He stretched his head up and stared wistfully off into the black sky. Almost reverently his little hands folded and rested across his knees. Softly, slowly, almost prayerfully, he whispered, "I wish I could be great." Seconds later he jerked to attention as if a commanding conscience had ordered him back to work. His eyes looked hopefully into mine as if seeking reassurance. What a thrill it was for me to tell him what I love to tell all human beings. "You can

137

be great, Jimmy. In fact, Mr. Wilson," I continued, "you are much greater than you think you are!"

I. HOW DO YOU BUILD SELF-LOVE IN YOUNG PEOPLE?

1. *Help them to see the importance of the seemingly unimportant.*

To the shoe-shine boy I said, "Jimmy, your job is far more important than you can begin to imagine." "But I can't be great—I'm only a shoe-shine boy," my friend Jimmy Wilson replied. "You have no idea how important your job is," I again challenged Jimmy. "When you shine shoes you give men greater confidence in their appearance, and with renewed confidence in their good grooming they leave this stand more self-reliant, enthusiastic and ambitious."

An enormous amount of inadequate self-worth stems from too low an estimate of our importance. We tend to measure value by rank, position and size. We forget that the mosquito halted the construction of the Panama Canal for years. The snowflake defeated Napoleon.

What is the most important part of an automobile? The motor? The battery? I suppose the tires wouldn't think they were important. The steering wheel? The spark plugs? The gas tank? The truth is that without any one of these parts the car would be useless.

Who is the most important man in the Army? The general? How far would he get without the private with a rifle at the front line? Is the infantryman the most important? Or is it the communications officer who gets the messages through? Perhaps it's the medical corpsman? No person will ever be able to accept his position in life until he sees this vital point: No job, no matter how insignificant and lowly, is less important than the entire project.

2. *Encourage the young person to discover and develop the unlimited potential that lies within.*

I counseled a young man who was tempted to drop out of college because, as he said, "I have a part-time job and they want me to work full time. They will pay me six hundred dollars a month!" That sounded like a fortune to him.

"Do you know," I said, "that if you'll take the next three years and complete college, you will earn far more than $7,200 a year for the following three years? If you will spend the next three years in college you will earn well over $300,000. That's $75,000 for each of four years in college."

"What do you mean?" he asked. I explained, "According to statistics the average college graduate earns $6,000 more a year in his forty years of earning power over the high school graduate. That means that if you complete college you will, in effect, be paid a total of $300,000 for three years of study. You might say that it's placed in a special bank account and will be returned to you at the rate of $6,000 a year for the next forty years." "Man!" he said. "I can't afford to drop out." He didn't.

Money, in and of itself, doesn't build real self-love. It can, however, be a very important tool in building self-esteem. A youngster who looks upon money only as a tool to buy big cars and expensive clothes in order to impress people so he can feed his self-worth is headed for trouble. But if he looks upon money as something he can use to help those in need and as something to educate and train himself and eventually his children, then it can become important in building self-love. For we love ourselves when we help others become what they should be.

Money builds hospitals. Money pays for scientific research which will heal the sick. Money is important. Every person owes it to himself and to society to earn the most money possible in the best possible way if he uses it for a real contribution to society.

3. *Never stop believing in the younger generation. Believe in your young people and let them know it.*

Jim Poppen rolled up an uninspiring high-school academic record. His parents were terribly concerned, but they never stopped believing in him. When he completed Hope Preparatory School, he decided he might like to become a doctor. Few people believed that he would make it. He enrolled in Medical School and really hit the books hard. At home on his first vacation, he told his parents how hard he was working. That night when everyone was asleep his father woke up and heard strange sounds in the kitchen. He stumbled through the darkness and was amazed to discover Jim sitting on the floor, tying knots in ropes that he had twisted from chair leg to chair leg.

"My boy's flipped! He just can't stand the pressure of study," Jim's father thought. When he expressed his astonishment and concern, the young student answered, "No, Dad, don't worry. I became interested in the human brain in medical school and made up my mind I'm going to become a brain surgeon. So my fingers are going to have to tie knots in areas where I'll be unable to see. I have to learn how to tie knots in the dark." Jim had discovered an area of interest that absolutely absorbed him.

All America was shocked when Robert F. Kennedy was shot. Driving to my office that morning, I heard a radio news report: "Dr. James Poppen, leading brain surgeon from Boston, Massachusetts, is flying to California to examine Robert F. Kennedy, who lies critically injured with a bullet in his brain."

Self-love is achieved when we discover the talent that God

140

has placed within us. There is unlimited potential in all young people. They are helped in discovering this potential when inspiring people—parents, teachers, ministers—dare to believe in today's youth.

II. HOW DO YOU BUILD SELF-LOVE IN THE DISADVANTAGED?

You build self-love in others by encouraging them to raise their achievement level. Self-love comes through self-improvement. Encourage people to become possibility thinkers. Help them to overcome their impossibility complex. Share with them the true stories of other people who have had every reason to amount to nothing because of physical handicaps or personal problems. Remind them that every problem is an opportunity in disguise. Every difficulty is a challenge to the human spirit to overcome it. That's the road to self-love.

There is the danger that, when we encounter those who have real problems or unusual hardships, we allow our sympathy for them to handicap us more than their problem handicaps them. Thus we are inclined to overly protect the sickly child and consequently restrain him from toughening himself for life. When we encounter those who have financial problems, we are inclined to give them money. More often than not, this kind of charity does more harm than good. John Wanamaker once was asked, "What's the hardest job in the world?" He answered, "How to give away money without doing more harm than good."

In our church work we have often encountered people in real financial difficulty. We used to give them money with no strings attached. Again and again we discovered that this was an affront to their self-dignity. In every case where our charity was generous, we eventually found ourselves alien-

141

ated from the recipients. First they began to depend upon our financial aid. This weakened their motivation for self-improvement. Then, when for their own good we discontinued giving the money, they became irate as if they were being cheated. Today we seldom give people money. We do *lend* money to people in need. We offer financial consultation at no charge.

Recently, a completely destitute young Mexican-American came to the church office. He was unable to work because he had sustained a back injury in an automobile accident. His wife was eight months pregnant. His little house was about to be foreclosed. After several interviews we helped him discover a possibility for achieving financial independence. We lent him enough to start a little business and meet his immediate obligations. We offered low interest and a long repayment period that he could meet. We lent him enough money to buy two incubators in which he could hatch quail eggs. He buys the eggs, hatches them, and sells the quail to hunting farms. As a result, he is proud of himself and, instead of being ashamed of facing us (as would have been the case if we had simply handed him a cash gift), he now comes to us proudly to report his progress and repay his loan.

You build self-love in others by helping them in the right way—and then not too much. In Whittier, California, Harward Stearns is an outstanding attorney. In his office, you are impressed with the way he listens intently and makes notes on a pad. What is fascinating is that he writes with an instrument that looks like a small cabinet knob with a nail protruding from its base. Then you notice that he is blind. He is taking notes in Braille. He is a senior partner in the law firm of Stearns, Gross and Moore. He remembers his childhood days when he was "sighted." He recalls his mother's face, the vivid sunsets and playing with little children. There

142

is absolutely no bitterness in his memories. "I was about twelve when I lost the sight of my right eye because of a detached retina. I knew it was only a question of time before the other eye would go. I remember accepting my fate and wondering how I would make out. My mother, however, had firm ideas. She is a fantastic woman.

"When I finally went totally blind at age thirteen, I stayed out of school only one semester. I made up that semester at home with the aid of my mother, who spent countless hours reading the lessons to me. I learned Braille.

"After high school, in Memphis, Tennessee, we moved to California and I was awarded a scholarship to Stanford University," Stearns said.

Recalling his first day at Stanford, Stearns told how he walked around with his mother to become acquainted with the campus. "I walked with the aid of a cane and felt I was fairly adept, but my mother knew I had a lot to learn. I came to a low curb, missed it and tripped. My mother didn't attempt to help me. She knew I would trip, and she permitted me this experience no matter what heartache it caused her. After all, she couldn't always be at my side and I had to learn."

Through college and law school, Stearns studied with the help of a battery of readers. He learned the standard and Braille typewriters and made an outline of every lecture. His efforts paid off, and he graduated Phi Beta Kappa.

Stearns's law practice has been "more than mildly successful."

While he feels no bitterness, the attorney admits he does have regrets. He regrets not being able to see his wife, Barbara, and their three children. But he is also grateful. "I've been very lucky. I've been helped with scholarships for my schooling and patient hours given by friends."

Stearns lives a full and useful life. He has been a trustee of the Lowell Joint School District and served as its president. He is active in the Lions Club, and has gone as high as deputy governor in that organization. He also takes part in the Whittier Area Joint Lions Sight Conservation Program, which purchases equipment to aid schools in teaching blind students. He has served as president of the Lions Eye Foundation of Southern California, Inc., and works with the Y-Indian Guides.

"I have a big debt to repay," Stearns explained, "and if I can do anything for a blind child, or any child for that matter, I feel it is just a small repayment on a large loan."

You build self-love in others when you encourage them to face their problems and turn them into personal triumphs!

You build self-love in others by giving them the freedom to discover themselves, to express themselves and to try. You must give them the freedom to win and the freedom to fail. Where there is no possibility of failure, there will be no possibility of self-discovery. For it is in trying that we find out what we are made of. We discover ourselves in our failures as much as we do in our successes. There is a profound verse in the Holy Bible which says, "And the eagle stirs up her nest that the young might learn to fly."

The sincere, sympathetic, compassionate person is oftentimes the greatest drawback to the building of self-love in his fellowman. We have discussed smotherly love, in which the mother is so protective that the child is never exposed to risks and can never discover the greatness within himself.

We can literally trap people in their own indignities by irresponsible charity. Mrs. Sarsadie Willis of East Liverpool, Ohio, begged for an opportunity to speak to the House of Representatives in Washington, D. C., about the problems of the poor. She wondered if they would give her the chance to

144

talk. They did. She began, "First, I am not a white racist talking, but a Negro woman who knows what she is talking about. So pay attention," Mrs. Willis admonished Democratic Representative Wayne L. Hayes in her opening paragraph. Then she spoke her piece: "Quit feeding people who won't work. Any human that gets something for nothing loses all pride of existence. Besides," she said, "there is always work to be done and it is cheaper to give people jobs than to hand out relief." At that point a rare thing happened—there was a loud general applause in the chambers, not only from the lawmakers from both sides of the aisle, but from the public galleries where such displays are contrary to House rules.

We build self-love in other people when we encourage them to assume and accept responsibility. Nobody will ever feel important if he doesn't have a responsible job. If he is not made to feel that he is responsible for himself, he will reach the lowest level of self-importance. Parents can teach self-love to their children by teaching them to assume responsibilities in their personal life and in their family circle.

"I am trying to teach my child responsibility, but that requires discipline. And my child resents discipline. What can I do?" a frustrated mother asked me. After listening to her for fifteen minutes, I concluded that she herself was very undisciplined. As an irresponsible adult, she did what she wanted to when she wanted to do it. Because she herself had had no father or mother to administer discipline, she had complete freedom to live the undisciplined life. I had to tell her, "Most childish resentment against discipline is a result of the parents' own undisciplined life. Parents have to live it before they can demand it. If we can comprehend this and apply it, we will see a reason behind an overwhelming amount of juvenile delinquency." This mother did not love herself!

145

No undisciplined, irresponsible person ever does. Children are not going to learn responsibility and they will never accept discipline from parents whom they see constantly "doing what they want to do, when they want to do it, the way they want to do it." But when they see self-discipline, self-restraint, self-imposed responsibility in their father and in their mother, they will accept discipline, restraint and responsibility in their own life.

III. HOW DO YOU BUILD SELF-LOVE IN OLD PEOPLE?

"The key word for the aged is 'self-esteem,' " said Dr. E. W. Busse, Jr., chairman of the Psychiatry Department at the Duke University Medical Center.

"Without self-esteem," he said, "they cannot maintain their health."

Dr. Busse, one of the nation's foremost authorities on aging, explains, "Our society, which has little appreciation for the nonachiever, must convince the elderly they are worthwhile and needed."

Dr. Busse is also director of the U.S. Public Health Service's Regional Center for the Study of the Aging. The center was founded in 1957, on the Duke campus, the first such unit in the nation.

Dr. Busse initiated a research project in 1954 on the relationship of various physiological, psychological and social factors to the aging process.

Some two hundred volunteers over sixty years of age have participated in this continuing program. Every three years the volunteers come to the center for two days of rigorous medical and psychological examinations.

The center is concerned with various aspects of aging, such as the changes that take place in the brain, the effects of various emotional states on body processes and the influence of physical slowdown on the social and psychological adjustment of the aged.

Dr. Busse, appointed to the U.S. Public Health National Advisory Child Health and Human Development Council, said the studies have shown there is no direct relationship between retirement and decline in health (and consequently death).

"But," he said, "there is evidence that the death rate for elderly persons increases shortly after admission to homes for the aged.

"It has long been known," Dr. Busse explained, "that social deprivation and hostile social influences have pathological consequences for infants.

"Now we know the same is true for the elderly. They must remain productive. Before retirement, an individual gained esteem by money, position, accomplishment. With these withdrawn, something must be found as a replacement.

"Therefore," Dr. Busse continued, "society has a responsibility to the aged. Society must supply the needed requirements—the opportunity for the elderly to contribute, praise for their work."

As advice to those nearing retirement, Dr. Busse said they first must face up to the situation, and then set definite goals for the years ahead.

"The aged," he said, "must remain active. You don't let a valuable machine rust."

An elderly resident of a home for the aged contributed this bit of advice which might help you build self-love in your aged friends:

Blessed are you who understand our faltering steps and shaking hands.

Blessed are you who know that our ears today must strain to catch the words you say.

Blessed are you who looked away when the coffee spilled on the table today!

Blessed are you who seem to know that our eyes are dim and our wits are slow.

Blessed are you who, with a cheery smile, stopped to chat with us for awhile.

Blessed are you who never say, when you come to visit— "You told me this story twice today."

Blessed are those who know the ways, who bring back memories of yesterdays, and

Blessed are you who make it known that we are being loved, respected, and are not really alone.

Remember that the aged feel guilty if they suspect they are a burden on their family or friends. How do you meet this problem? Teach them possibility thinking! The possibility-thinking person, no matter what his age or physical capabilities may be, knows that if he is a cheerful, uncomplaining, happy, twinkling personality, he will never be a burden to anyone. The joy-producing, happiness-spreading, enthusiasm-generating person is always a great source of spiritual strength. He's not just taking—he's giving! It's the grumbling, self-pitying, self condemning person who is a burden to those around him.

IV. HOW DO YOU BUILD SELF-LOVE IN THE HELPLESS?

Bill is twenty-one years old, and suffering from a severe case of epilepsy. When I called on him, he rose drowsily from his bed and said, "Let's go to the lounge and talk there." As he walked past the nurse's station he suddenly fell flat on his face. He lay motionless on the floor as the red blood from his face flowed across the white tiles and nurses rushed to lift him into a wheelchair. I waited for thirty minutes while they nursed his wounds. I was deeply touched by the obvious interest and affection of the nurse who bandaged the gash on his head.

Finally, when we were in the lounge, he began to talk, when suddenly another seizure gripped him. I helped him in the chair to keep him from falling. I waited while the tormenting tremor passed. Down the hall I could hear an insane patient shouting unspeakable obscenities. Finally, Bill turned his blue eyes to mine and stumbled out the question. "What is the purpose of all this, Reverend? When I was very young I wanted to be a Dr. Tom Dooley, helping people. But look at me. I'm helpless." I prayed silently and answered, "Bill, among the kinds of people in this world—there are helpful people and helpless people. But the helpless often help the helpful. I saw how that nurse loved you as she bandaged your wounds a minute ago. For thirty minutes you made her feel important and needed! These nurses take paychecks home to feed and clothe their children. Believe me, the helpless are helping more than they will ever know." I'll never forget the look in his eyes. For the first time in his life he could love himself, knowing that he, too, was causing a worthy contribution to be made to the human family.

V. HOW DO YOU BUILD SELF-LOVE IN THOSE WHO WORK FOR YOU?

Follow the advice in the early part of this chapter about the importance of each person being made to realize the vital importance of the most menial work.

In addition, generate an atmosphere of enthusiasm and

mutual understanding. Unbelievable tension, jealousy and resentment are developed in many organizations by executives who just don't have the common sense to work at the business of building self-love in their employees and in their associates.

One summer while on a Mediterranean cruise I met the head of a great American industrial firm. "You must, at times," I said, "feel the beginning of jealousy or resentment when some of your executives succeed to the point where they may threaten your own position. How do you handle that?" I'll never forget his answer. Quietly, calmly, with twinkling eyes, he said, "It's very simple. I could allow myself to become jealous or fearful through insecurity, but I know that if I did, this would give rise to resentment. Resentment would break our communications. Deterioration would set in. I could of course fire the guy and be rid of him, but I would lose a valuable man for the company. The company would suffer and, as a result, I would suffer even though I had satisfied my arrogance and pride."

I sat looking at this strong, self-assured man as he leaned forward and said, "Here's my secret. Some people say, 'Live and let live.' My philosophy is, 'Live—let live—live off.' "

I must have looked a little shocked, because he explained, "When I take a live-and-let-live attitude, everything goes better. Profits go up. The departments show greater success. And the Board of Directors is thrilled with the great job the President and the Chairman of the Board are doing! So, in a sense, I am living off what others are doing. Meanwhile, I have an enormous sense of self-respect because I know that I am giving my men the freedom to rise as high as they possibly can. I benefit from it emotionally and I benefit from it financially. I teach this to key people in the company. It works wonders!"

150

VI. BUILD SELF-LOVE IN EVERYONE THROUGH THE USE OF THESE MAGIC SENTENCES

I AM SORRY.

This sentence builds self-love because it helps a person whom you have wronged to know that he isn't so bad after all and that you are not perfect yourself. Don't be afraid to expose your own imperfections. The father, the mother, the teacher, the minister of a church, the professor in the classroom—all have an image of perfection to those who look up to them. It does wonders to honestly let those around you know that you are not perfect in your decision making, in the exercise of discipline and in private and public life.

I APPRECIATE YOU.

This is another magic sentence for building self-love in others. We tend to be so busy, so preoccupied with our projects, that we don't take enough time to express our gratitude. Every individual needs periodic reassurance. A certain amount of self-esteem leaks out of one's life if he feels that he is being taken for granted.

YOU WERE RIGHT: I WAS WRONG.

Another magic sentence that builds self-worth in and around us is an admission like that. We know that it takes a big man to admit that he was wrong. Why? Because a big man feels deeply secure within himself. He's the kind of man who can safely admit his error. If you dare not say, "You were right. I was wrong," it indicates that you have to do some pretty serious work on building your own self-trust.

I'M NOT SURE ABOUT THIS—WHAT DO YOU THINK WE OUGHT TO DO?

This is another magic sentence that builds self-love in those around you. It implies that you believe they are intelligent. The suggestion box in modern institutions and

151

industrial firms is enormously valuable too in building up the self-esteem of the average person.

All of these sentences make the other man feel that he is a Person—and not just a tool.

Most important, *you build self-love when you teach that greatness depends more on character than on achievement.* Probably 99 per cent of all human beings tend to measure their importance and their value and their worth by their productivity. Nothing could be farther from the truth as far as our society is concerned. In a Communist society, the worth of a person depends upon his productivity.

If this were so, the housewife would consider herself insignificant doing menial household tasks. She cleans and washes, and twenty-four hours later has nothing to show for her time and labor. She would begin to feel that she is on a meaningless, thankless, noncreative merry-go-round. Her husband comes home from work with tales of personal accomplishment. Other women are seemingly accomplishing so much more in their lifetime. The housewife may plunge into deep periods of depression stemming from lack of self-love unless she understands the greatest lesson of all: *It's not what you do—it's what you are!*

Dr. Raymond Beckering, one of the ministers on my staff, was the pastor of a church in Chicago. One day he received a call from the wife of a famous doctor who said, "My husband, Dr. Cornelius VerMeulen, has had a heart attack. Would you be willing to make a pastoral call in the hospital?" On the way to the hospital, Dr. Beckering wondered what he could possibly say to such a great person. He prayed. When he entered the hospital room, he saw the doctor sitting up in bed.

"Dr. Beckering, how happy I am to see you! I have something wonderful to share with you," the famed urologist said.

"I have had a supreme discovery while I have been confined to this bed." His eyes sparkled. His face was radiant. Vitality, life radiated from his face. With the speechless pastor, the doctor shared his exciting discovery. "I've discovered that it's not what you do—it's what you are that matters in life."

As a result, the doctor committed his life to Jesus Christ. He continued his rise to eminence as one of the foremost urologists in the world. But his enormous sense of self-respect and self-love comes through living the Christian life of love, joy and peace.

Any person—no matter what his position, age or physical condition—has the capacity to *be* a wonderful person!

WHAT DOES THE WORLD NEED MORE THAN ANYTHING ELSE TODAY?

It doesn't seem to be more technical knowledge. We build rockets, we solve scientific problems and we transplant human organs. What do we need more than all of this? We need brotherhood, understanding and love. The world desperately needs the Spirit of Christ. You can make yourself into the kind of person who can spread this love around. Nothing can be more important in the world than that. And when you know that you are a faith-building, cheer-spreading, hope-generating, encouragement-offering person, you will know how wonderful you are. Teach people this truth, and you build self-love within them.

WHAT HAPPENS WHEN WE BUILD SELF-LOVE IN OTHERS?

We discover that we reap the greatest reward possible for ourselves as an unexpected by-product. We discover that we love ourselves in the process! One of my very good friends,

Walter Knott, the founder of the world-famed Knott's Berry Farm, is a Christian capitalist. He is driven by the profit motive. But deeper than this profit motive is a human dignity-creating motive.

"The answer to our poverty problems," says Mr. Knott, "is to create job opportunities that men might earn their own expenses through life and walk home on Friday night with a check in their pocket, and dignity in their soul!" Mr. Knott lives very modestly. He told me one day, "I could move out of this simple little apartment where my wife and I live. I could buy a big new car. But I find more joy in investing my profits in my business. By so doing I create new job opportunities."

The famous founder of this multimillion-dollar tourist attraction proudly declares, "I need about $7,000 in net profits to create one new job opportunity. Once I was tempted to buy a home in Newport for $140,000. Then I began to think—I could sink this back into the farm and create twenty new job opportunities! So that's what I did. What a joy it is for me to open up these new businesses and watch some person find the joy of a wonderful job that can give him the pride he deserves. My greatest satisfaction in life is knowing that some widow, some young person or some human being who has been discriminated against can come here and find an honest job and win the biggest prize life has to offer—self-respect."

Build self-love in others—and you build self-love in yourself! *You will love yourself without really trying.*

154

X

HOW TO REBUILD A SHATTERED
SELF-LOVE

What do you do when you lose your self-esteem? How do you rebuild a faltering self-confidence? How do you recover a lost sense of self-worth? How do you rebuild a shattered self-love?

For twenty years I have counseled people who, though once self-reliant and easygoing, experienced embarrassing difficulties which resulted in the collapse of their self-assurance.

Mary, a bride-to-be, had already mailed the invitations to her wedding. Her dress and the gowns of her four attendants were already purchased. The wedding cake, baked and frosted, was waiting to be cut the following day. She was wrapping her gift for the groom when the telephone rang. It was he! "Mary," the voice was strained. "Hi, John, aren't you excited?" she asked. "Mary," he continued painfully, "I can't go through with it. I mean it's all off. There isn't going to be a wedding tomorrow. Don't ask questions. I'm sorry. Good-bye."

Now the stunned young woman sat in her pastor's office. "What is wrong with me? I know there must be something terribly wrong in my life." Her slender shoulders trembled as her head dropped. "I'm so embarrassed. I can't face anyone anymore. Somewhere, I failed terribly."

I have heard virtually the same words from a man who had just come through a divorce; from the mother of three children whose husband had quietly deserted her; from a millionaire who suffered financial reverses and subsequent bankruptcy; from an executive who was mysteriously "let go" from a firm he had served faithfully for years; and from more alcoholics than I can remember.

When these kinds of life situation hit and you feel inept and unsure of yourself, you can recapture lost confidence. You can have a rebirth of self-worth. A way out and up is always possible.

Reconstruction always begins with controlled thinking. You must learn to distinguish between negative and positive thinking; between death-dealing thoughts and life-giving thoughts. Thoughts of resentment, self-flagellating thoughts, thoughts of vengeance will destroy the undamaged goodness that remains within you.

I. CONTROL YOUR IMMEDIATE REACTION

It is important to realize that if you cannot change what has happened, you can control how you react to what has happened. Remember that you will never again be the person you were before you experienced this trauma. You may react negatively and become less worthy. Or you may react positively—and become better than ever. You can become an impossibility thinker: "I have nothing to live for anymore. I hate myself." Then you will really go on the skids. Or you can choose to be a possibility thinker: "I have failed, but I am still a person of worth." Follow this mental road and you'll find a new life.

II. RESTRAIN THE RUNAWAY SELF-RECRIMINATING THOUGHTS

Self-debasing thoughts will come naturally to your mind. Restrain them. Whatever you do—do not believe them. They are extreme, emotional exaggerations. By all means, resist the destructive inclination to welcome, nurse, feed and strengthen these self-destroying feelings. The depressed person tends to strengthen his self-debasing thinking by deliberately choosing to believe the worst about himself. He deliberately goes on a self-degrading mental rampage: listing all the failures he has ever encountered; pointing up all the weaknesses in his life; recalling from his long forgotten past any and every blunder he has ever made. In this crazy, self-destroying mental activity, he

(1) exaggerates the significance and the reality of these real or forceful shortcomings;

(2) blames himself almost entirely and mercilessly for all these failures, stubbornly refusing to believe or remember how other persons contributed to his mistakes;

(3) forget or rudely discredits any and all of his worthy virtues and accomplishments. He belittles, berates and betrays the noble qualities of his character. He angrily scorns the value or the reality of all the positive qualities in his life when some friend calls them to his attention.

Why do we tend to despair and further degrade ourselves

with self-destructive thinking? Are we seeking sympathy to nurse our wounded pride? Do we hate ourselves so much that we want to mentally liquidate, eliminate and eradicate that which we hate? Does an irrational subconscious suppose that it will love itself if it mentally destroys the self it hates? Or are we trying to atone for the guilt of failure? Do we deliberately inflict this mental punishment upon ourselves, hoping to finally awaken feeling that we are redeemed through the crucifixion of self-condemnation? Whatever the reason—know this—it is important to understand that you cannot rebuild self-love by destroying the undamaged areas of self-worth that still remain.

III. WATCH OUT FOR SELF-PITY

You certainly do not rebuild self-love by indulging in self-pity. Self-pity does not generate self-respect. Self-pity focuses on the unhappy past, keeping alive the very experiences which must be forgotten and left behind. Self-pity focuses on what has happened. While you are concentrating on the unfortunate past, you are in that moment enslaved, controlled and dominated by that self-demoralizing past. When you recall the past, you are at that moment recaptured by it. It may have happened, but don't allow yourself to remain trapped in that experience by self-pity.

"Forgetting these things that are behind—I press toward the mark," Paul wrote. If unpleasant things come to pass— by all means let them do so. Why are we so inclined to self-pity? Are we trying to tenderly nurse a wounded self-love? If so, we must see that self-pity only keeps the wounded pride raw and open. In our own self-pity we hope to gain the pity of others, mistaking sympathy for respect. We crave to reassure the faltering self that it is worthy after all. If we feel this way, we must understand that pity is not necessarily respect. Sympathy is not necessarily esteem. Or do we indulge in self-pity—trapping ourselves in the past—for fear of moving ahead into a future where we might suffer additional assaults? Is self-pity a deceptive defense mechanism willfully experienced to protect me from the new risks I may encounter if I start thinking of beginning again? You will never rebuild self-love until you *liberate yourself from the tyranny of unpleasant memories.* You are on the way when you stop thinking and talking about them. *Do not allow them to control you.* Banish thoughts such as "I'm finished. . . . I am a failure. . . . I'll never do anything worthwhile. . . . I bungled every chance I had. . . . I hate myself. . . . I'll never amount to anything."

1. *Failure is no disgrace.* "Not failure but a low aim is a crime." At least you had the courage to try. It is more honorable to try something worthwhile and fail than never to attempt any worthy venture. Play-it-safe people seldom win the applause and the respect of others—they never do anything to merit congratulations!

2. *Failure is proof that I'm a human being.* Tell yourself that if I have suffered failure, I am in good company. I can be sure I am a member of the human race. Every person has failed sometime, somewhere, even if it was the failure to see and seize a great opportunity. That often is the most costly, albeit unrevealed, failure.

3. *Failure can be fruitful.* If my failures teach me something, they will not be without positive value. I can learn my weaknesses. I can learn something about other people or, if nothing more, I can learn patience, compassion and humility

through my failure. This failure may turn out to be the greatest thing that ever happened to me.

4. *Failure never needs to be final.* A friend sent me a letter at the turn of the year. She wrote, "I haven't failed this year —I just haven't succeeded yet." How different from another person, who said: "I've failed at marriage—how I hate myself." "Because you have failed in *a* marriage," I counseled, "it does not follow that you have permanently failed in *marriage.* Believe that you can have a new marriage someday. And feeling this, you will become the cheerful kind of person whom someone will find desirable. Then you can make your next marriage a great success with the help of God." This advice proved to be prophetic. He has a very successful second marriage today.

5. *Failure is never total.* "I'm a complete failure," the self-degrading person wrongly claims. No person is ever a total failure.

Any person who claims he is completely worthless is absolutely wrong. The late Dr. Smiley Blanton, an eminent psychiatrist, once said to his colleague Norman Vincent Peale, "There are vast undamaged areas in every human life. These undamaged areas must be discovered, then used as the base for a new beginning."

Psychiatrists have long noted that mental illness never seems to be total. Freud wrote that even patients with severe hallucinations later reported that "in some corner of their minds, as they express it, there was a normal person hidden, who watched the progress of the illness go past like a detached spectator."

In World War II an asylum in France that housed 158 persons considered hopelessly and incurably insane was liberated by advancing armies. All the inmates escaped. Years

160

later it was discovered that fifty-three were living normal lives, apparently completely recovered.

No matter what your condition—you can rebuild a meaningful future. You can reconstruct a self-love–generating life.

IV. BUILD A BOLSTERING BELIEF

Build a bolstering belief. Richard Lemon, in an article entitled "The Uncertain Science," offers a brilliant survey of all popular forms of psychiatric therapy—psychoanalysis, psychotherapy, chemotherapy, group therapy, milieu therapy —and concludes, "Confidence and belief are the most dramatic factors that affect mental health."

You can rebuild your shattered self-love, but it will likely be a slow step-by-step process. Dr. Walter E. Alvarez, in his book *Minds that Came Back*, makes this statement: "Most emotionally induced illness does not come as the result of one large emotion. Far more often it is the result of the monotonous drip, drip, drip of seemingly unimportant emotions—the everyday run of anxiety—fear—disappointments and longings. There is no set point where one is suddenly into the land of emotional illness. What is critical is the daily pattern of behavior." Likewise, the recovery of mental health often comes through the daily, constant exposure of the mind to the kind of positive thoughts that will slowly but surely build confidence and belief.

Affirm—out loud—"I am a normal human being!" This will produce two benefits.

1. It will gradually remove the self-condemnation from your mind. The fact that you have suffered rejection, injustice, embarrassment, failure, or a mental breakdown

161

under stress does not mean you are an unworthy person—it only proves you are human. In World War II, if a man caved in under combat stress, he might be court-martialed. Then, in the last days of the war, the 8th Air Force in England discovered that even the heroes, after enough missions, began to have nervous convulsions, to "begin to come apart at the seams."

2. A second benefit will result from the discovery of your humanness. You will become more authentically humble. You will admit to the normal need for self-improvement. You will be ready to accept constructive help.

A man who lost all self-love, to the point of considering suicide, came for counseling. He was arrogant, haughty, proud and desperate. Recovering from his depression, he writes, "I am acutely aware now of my weaknesses, limitations and shortcomings, of those areas of my personality which require reformation—because I am human! And as facetious as it may sound, that simple fact, that stark realization, is the singularly most important truth which I faced in 1968. That I was not superhuman, that I was but the equal of man, that I was not sainted, nor marked by 'destiny' for unearthly accomplishments. They have become the touchstones for a life plan which I had never before understood. I can now identify my personal worth and dignity, because I realize I am a human being. I have been forced to develop realistic goals, ambitions and levels of aspirations commensurate with existing abilities. I have stripped away my lofty pretenses. And despite the vulnerability of this new nakedness, my assuaged ego has spawned self-respect."

This man, who has gained insight, is rapidly on the road to recovering a real self-esteem. In his words: "No, Bob, I

162

have not yet experienced a full cure, let alone a quick cure. The instantaneous conversion from 'I hate myself—I'm ill' to 'I love myself—I'm well' is as unscientifically unsound as the expectation of rain from a cloudless sky. As the days passed since that terribly dark day when I determined suicide, I have come to hate myself less. And as the imprisoning slice of self-hatred peeled away, an undercore of positive values was liberated."

He has come a long way already. He now writes clearly of the depth of his self-hate: "It was another world, sunken beyond measure. It was lonely, dark, frightening, moribund. A satanic kingdom where the ear is keyed to the pitch of ridicule, ostracism, isolation and banishment. Sad ear, once deaf to the clouded pleasantry of distorted reality, now alive and quick to the cacophony of unreality mutilated.

nodreamNodreamNoDreamNODREAM! ! ! ! ! ! ! ! ! ! ! !
mustdieMustdieMustDieMUSTDIE! ! ! ! ! ! ! ! ! ! ! !
realityRealityReAlItyREALITY! ! ! ! ! ! ! ! ! ! ! !

"In case anyone should ask you, tell them I'm back. You may say, further, that I am just as loud and I'm still kicking, but make no mistake—I am back!" He concluded his written report to me with: "Do I still have lofty goals? Of course, only now I'm proud of them—God shared in their selection. What are my motives and methods? No more and no less than the simple answers to simple prayers. That's right— real answers to real prayers. The reason? I changed '*My* will be done' to '*Thy* will be done.' Do I still experience failures? I certainly do. I have found this especially to be true each time I attempted to compete with God. Am I now able to relate to others? Well, not all the time. I have noticed, though, that the more I keep my mouth shut and give God's a chance to speak, the more people seem to listen. Any fears? That's hard to answer. I don't fear yesterday, that's done with; nor tomorrow, and most certainly not today—Now—that's the place in time I call home, remember?

"Quite imperfectly, I'm trying to describe a state of happiness. Grammatically phrased, what I've written doesn't end with a period but a colon; believe me, there's more to follow. The New Year tastes like a breath of fresh air. Just give me a chance to catch my second wind and then watch My Partner and me make molehills out of mountain tops."

You too can make a comeback! Affirm: "I am a worthy person. I am a human being. God loves human beings— especially those who want and need His help."

V. LET YOUR TROUBLE LEAD YOU CLOSER TO GOD

Affirm: "I believe in God. I have tried to live without Him. I have suffered, but I shall use my suffering constructively. I shall let it turn me to a belief in God."

I received a letter from a remarkable man who generously expressed his appreciation for my book *Move Ahead with Possibility Thinking*. He is Ben Franklin, of Topeka, Kansas, whose inspiring conquest of misfortune was published in the *Christian Athlete* in November 1968. Ben enjoyed mountain climbing:

"Climbing was my exaltation; summits were my world. Nothing seemed auspicious about April 14, 1963. I'd had minor falls in the past; once a rope gashed my lower back when stopping a fellow camper in a practice fall. I was climbing with two other fellows, Paul Porter and Gerald Childers, freshmen like myself at the University of Colorado. We had spent the afternoon practicing on the walls of the Amphitheatre, a small rock formation near Boulder. While I was on the last pitch of a particularly difficult ascent I slipped, my rope broke on a jagged ridge separating me from my 'belayer' and I fell 150 feet to the base of the cliff. Paul and Gerald were, fortunately, left unhurt up on a high ledge. Using a spare rope, they got down to me as fast as they could.

"My back was broken in four places, my pelvis in two . . . but I was still breathing. Gerald stayed with me while Paul ran to get help. By this time I was only half-conscious. Everything seemed black around me. The only thing I remember thinking, over and over, was the one unendurable question: 'What happened to my rope?' How long it was before Paul returned, I don't know. He had with him a rescue squad and a stretcher. Completely delirious by now, I was lifted onto the stretcher, strapped tighty and carried down the canyon to a waiting ambulance. Time seemed remote as it sped the thirty miles to Denver with siren screaming. . . .

"I had been paralyzed from the waist down.

"The ensuing weeks in the hospital were filled by prayer, pain and angry tears. I couldn't move my legs! I had spent nine years climbing on those legs, but a split-second fall had emptied them of power! Three weeks passed with no return of motion. Four weeks; my legs wouldn't budge. I was consumed by grief and rage. Discouragement crowded the hours. An enormous sense of futility and despair engulfed me. I kept asking myself 'Why?' Why had I gone climbing that day? Why had that rope broken? Why couldn't I move my legs? Why hadn't God done something to help me? Why? Why? Why?

"One operation was performed and then another, but to no

avail. My spinal cord had been too badly damaged when my back was broken. I was told I would have to use a wheelchair. And I spent day after panic-filled day, watching the motionless sheets in horror.

"*There comes a time in every man's life when he is scared,* so scared that he is forced to realize just how insignificant he is before life's awesome might. Brains, ability and strength all fail him in such a moment. Power and prestige fail him. He can bare himself in prayer to Almighty God, asking His help and imploring His forgiveness. With faith he can hear God's answers.

"And so it was for me. *For the first real time in my life, I knew without doubt that I needed God. I needed Him unquestioningly and unashamedly.* I was terrified. Four weeks had passed since my mountain-climbing accident, and I was still flat on my back with my lower body useless. My legs were growing smaller by the day and time was running out. If I didn't move those legs soon, I would never move them. The doctors and therapists told me as much.

"Before the accident my relationship to Christ was all one way—Him to me. For my part I didn't care one way or the other. My belief was merely a cursory one in God, which I didn't bother to keep open much of the time. This all changed. I began to pray—and to understand. I began to be thankful, even then, for blessings I had never noticed before—for family, friends, beauty, the love of God and Christ, for life itself.

"Five weeks passed, and six weeks. There was no sign of return. But then it came . . . six weeks and a few hours after my plunge down the face. I moved a toe! Suddenly all the pain and torture of those terror-filled weeks was washed away in the blinding realization that God had seen fit to answer

166

my prayers and those of my friends in this manner. I had moved a toe! With tears streaming down my face, and thankfulness spilling from my heart, I called my parents to let them know the ordeal was over. I was no longer totally paralyzed. Now recovery could begin.

"Almost five years have passed since that joyful night in a Denver rehabilitation hospital. I re-entered the University of Colorado in September of 1963, attending classes in a wheelchair. To wean myself from the doggone chair I planned a trip to Europe in 1964 and left the chair behind when I got on the plane in New York City. The first two weeks on crutches were rugged but I'm still using them. I graduated from Colorado in 1967, one semester late. I was able to make the dean's list four of the five semesters, take part in extra-curricular activities (a yearbook editor, lecture series chairman, etc.) and was among 30 students in CU's 15,000 named to *Who's Who Among Students in American Universities and Colleges*. I've been to Europe and Iceland since my accident and this past summer traveled around the world, visiting Iron Curtain countries as I had in 1964—and appreciating America much more as the result.

"There's no chance I'll ever fully recover. I have 50 per cent use of my my left leg, 25 per cent use of the right. Each year I get around a little better, using crutches, leg braces and a back brace.

"But every day of these last few years has had an abundance of beauty in it, and every day has had many reasons to be thankful. *I now think that I fell into the hands of God, rather than from them on that day in the mountains. And as much as I would like to walk normally again, I wouldn't give all the possessions I own for the blessings I've enjoyed.*

"I never drive my car on the highways, some 60,000 miles

each year, without asking His blessing and expressing my gratitude. For I gained a richer understanding of God's abundant life through my accident.

"I've learned that if we will just look through our eyes with God, we'll find peace and energy and love and power beyond belief. We'll find the answers for which we've been searching. And with God's help, our lives can be rich, full and inexpressibly beautiful.

"I know. God's summits of blessings are now my world."

If you have suffered a severe fall—a broken marriage, a lost job, financial reverse, rejection by a dear friend—let yourself drop into the hands of God and you will find the faith to come alive again.

XI

GIVE YOURSELF A SELF-IMAGE TRANSPLANT

If all of the suggestions in this book have failed to give you a new sense of self-worth, it probably means that your self-image is so damaged that you need a new self-image transplanted into your mind.

The world was thrilled and joyous when the news was beamed from South Africa that Dr. Christian Barnard had performed the first successful heart transplant. I have good news for you! You can undergo a self-image transplant!

Dr. Maxwell Maltz, in his book *Psycho-Cybernetics*, has described how people who underwent plastic surgery suddenly developed an exciting new self-image. They began to believe in their new attractiveness. They began to love themselves. Their lives and personalities were radically transformed.

In a similar way hundreds of human beings acquire new self-images through the power of prayer. I myself have been practicing the technique of prayer for almost forty years and have used it therapeutically with sick and troubled people for more than twenty years. I can report that I do not know of a single person who failed when he honestly and faithfully prayed in the manner I shall describe.

Most critics of prayer are people who have never tried it long enough to be reliable reporters. Many others who try to invalidate the spiritual power of prayer don't go about it in the right way. I recall reading that a native in Africa, upon seeing a small transistor radio, pounded it against a rock shouting, "Talk! Talk, talk, talk to me! They said you could talk." His problem was that he didn't know how to turn it on and tune it in. In his ignorance, he was demolishing and discarding a really effective tool.

I have counseled with hundreds of people who were frustrated and anxiety-ridden. They ignored the power of prayer and considered it a fantasy—until they learned how to pray effectively.

It has been scientifically proved that effective prayer does perform miracles in human personality.

A prominent psychiatrist has written: "Speaking as a student of psychotherapy whose subject is generally unconcerned with theology, I am convinced that the Christian religion is one of the most valuable and potent influences for producing harmony and peace of mind needed to bring health and power to a large proportion of nervous patients. In some cases I have attempted to cure nervous patients with suggestions of quietness and confidence but without success until I linked these suggestions to faith in the power of God and prayer, which is the substance of Christian belief. And then the patient became strong."

Dr. Alexis Carrell, a Nobel prize–winning medical doctor, wrote in a paper published posthumously, "Prayer is not only worship. It is also an invisible emanation of man's worshiping spirit. The most perfect form of energy that one can generate. The influence of prayer upon the human mind and body is as demonstrable as that of any secreting gland. Its results can be measured in terms of increased physical buoyancy, greater intellectual vigor, moral stamina and a deeper understanding of the realities that underlie human relationships. In fact, I would say, true prayer is a way of life, the truest life is literally a prayer."

You can believe scientists—prayer can work the miracle of creating a new and lovable self within you!

Few people have demonstrated a greater self-redeeming love than St. Francis of Assisi. Once a Florentine nobleman said to him, "I have one question to ask you. What is your secret?" St. Francis answered, "It is prayer. Prayer. And, it is prayer!"

There are millions of people who have found how to live with themselves and enjoy it when they discovered Jesus Christ. What was the secret of the great self-confidence, self-assurance and self-affection that was evidenced in Jesus Christ? It was His in-touchness with God through prayer.

AN EXAMPLE OF THE POWER OF PRAYER

One hundred million miracles happen every day through prayer. There are circumstances that occur through prayer than can only be explained in terms of the miraculous. A friend of mine, Herb Wallace, is pastor of the Church of God in Garden Grove, California. As the new church structure was being completed, he ran into a financial snag with the contractor. It appeared that the congregation might lose twenty thousand dollars to the builder, who was not prepared to provide this amount of service which they believed he should. Finally, the church hired an attorney. As Herb tells it, "The attorney was wonderful, but he didn't have a big enough name to influence the attorney who represented the contractor. We were just not getting to first base in this situation. I was so frustrated and anxious about it that I thought I was going to crack up. All I could do was pray, 'God, guide me and help me.' I prayed for guidance and guess what thought came into my mind? 'Why don't you go fishing, Herb?'

"Now that seemed like a peculiar thing for God to advise. But at least it would relax me. So I put my boat on its trailer, attached it to my car and drove out to the Salton Sea. As I drove through the desert I kept praying, 'God, what can I do about my problem?' That prayer was answered as the following thoughts flowed through my mind. I remembered that every time I had gone to the Salton Sea I would see some poor people from Los Angeles fishing at the end of the pier, catching the little ones. They couldn't afford a boat to go out into deeper waters where the big fish were lying. God seemed to be saying to me now, 'Herb Wallace, stop worrying about yourself. Start thinking about others. Take your boat and drive out to the end of the pier and if you see any of those poor folks out there fishing, offer to take them out in your boat to catch some really good fish. Forget about yourself.'

"I reached the Salton Sea and launched the boat. I sailed it to the end of the pier. To my astonishment nobody was fishing there. But I did see a very well-dressed man sitting there with his wife. I was inclined to ignore them until he called out, 'How about a ride?' I pulled alongside the pier which gave him a chance to explain. 'We drove out from

Palm Springs, tried to rent a boat out here, but found none were available. I'd love to see the sea. I wonder if you'd be willing to rent your boat to me.' I replied, 'I won't rent it to you, but I'll be glad to give you a ride. I'm all alone anyway. Come on.' "

As they rode around the lake Herb began talking about his church.

"Before I knew it I was telling this fellow about my problem. I said, 'We've got a lawyer but he doesn't have a big enough name to get the contractor's attorney moving. If I had an outstanding lawyer I know we could lick our problem.' "

The unexpected guest sitting in the bow of the boat in his luxurious gray flannel suit startled Reverend Wallace by saying, "I know where you can get such an attorney." He took out his business card and handed it to Herb Wallace. If I could divulge his name, I am sure you would recognize it. He is world-famous, one of the highest-priced lawyers in the world, representing celebrities in America and England.

Herb was dumbfounded. "I don't think I could begin to afford to hire you," Herb said. The celebrated attorney replied, "For goodness sakes, Reverend Wallace, I could buy and sell your church building and earn less than I have earned on many a fee. I'll be glad to work for nothing, providing you won't tell anyone that I have. That is, if you don't mind having a Jew represent you on church business." Herb Wallace replied, enthusiastically and promptly, "Well, as I remember, Jesus Christ was a Jew. And he was represented by a few Jews named Peter, James and John. I don't see why I should have any objections. Thanks a million."

The following day this celebrated lawyer shot off a letter

173

to the contractor's attorney, who proceeded to comply with the conditions of contract promptly and forthrightly.

I have no doubt that if you could calculate all of the potential odds against such a meeting between this minister and the lawyer, you would have to conclude that such an event would be virtually a mathematical improbability. I can only conclude that it was very definitely a miraculous answer to prayer.

Try prayer power, and solve your biggest problems. Through prayer you can learn to live with yourself and love yourself.

There's a right way and a wrong way to pray. I would like to share with you six steps to effective prayer which I guarantee will give you a new self-image.

To help you to better remember these six steps after you've closed this book, I have arranged the six thoughts in this acrostic:

PRAYER IS

1. **P**ursuing God.
2. **R**eexamination of self.
3. **A**ffirming positively what God is doing within you.
4. **Y**ielding your self-will to Christ.
5. **E**xpecting positive results. Real prayer expects great things to happen—and great things do.
6. **R**ejoicing—prayer is thanking God for what you are, what He has done for you, and what He will do for you.

Let's look at these six steps to self-image–transplanting power.

I. PURSUING GOD

Prayer is a natural instinct of man in which the human soul reaches out for the God-Reality.

When God wanted to provide animals with lifesaving reactions, He gave them instincts. Man has been provided with an instinct to reach out for a spiritual power beyond himself. Prayer is an inborn, intuitive inclination to pursue something greater than ourselves.

Prayer, then, is not the product of human neurosis. I am well aware that there are psychoanalysts who have suggested that religion is rooted in fear, something invented by anxiety-ridden human beings in the dawn of history.

Let me address myself to this concept. First, there is abundant evidence to point out that primitive religions were not rooted in fear, but rather in a sense of awe and wonderment. The ancient Egyptians, for instance, did not worship objects of fear. They worshiped the beetle and the jackal. If their primitive religion had been rooted in fear, they would have worshiped the objects of their fear. I cannot accept the irresponsible thesis of some psychiatrists and anthropologists who tell us that religion had its origin in fear.

The urge to run to God in time of fear, anxiety, strain or stress is spiritual intuition planted in the human being by the Almighty Creator—in order that we might never forsake Him. The same power that plants within the salmon the mysterious compulsion to return to its place of birth, has placed within the human animal the spiritual compulsion to return to his original source of spiritual life. On the first level, then, prayer is a primitive pursuit after the God who made us.

175

Traveling on the plane to London, I sat next to a psychiatrist from New York. I posed this question to her: "What's the difference between man and other animals?" She replied, "My professor in Warsaw used to say, 'The difference between man and other animals is that man knows there's a God. Animals don't.' " It is indeed a fact that of all of the animals on planet earth, only one animal reaches out for God, only one has demonstrated a universal spiritual hunger for God, only one has professed to have had contact with this God in prayer. That animal happens to be the most rational, most intelligent and brilliant of all creatures. Prayer is implanted in man by the Creative Power.

Lillian Roth, in her deeply moving book, *I'll Cry Tomorrow*, described her soul struggles. She tells us that she was never able to conquer her problem until she uttered three words—three of the hardest words she could ever speak— "I NEED HELP." In the struggle to rebuild a self-image we will probably never succeed until we take the first step of prayer—until we cry out, "GOD—I NEED HELP."

II. REEXAMINATION OF SELF

Reexamination of the self is the second step to effective prayer. The second phase of spiritual surgery that can effect a self-image transplant calls for an honest self-appraisal. This is probably the hardest thing for any human being. We are all inclined to be overpowered by conscious and subconscious guilt feelings which would keep us from moving close enough to God for Him to perform the spiritual miracle.

While we have an intuition to approach God, at the same time we also feel guilty lest we be exposed as the frauds that we often are and find ourselves rejected by God and consequently by ourselves. *Doubt then becomes a subconscious defensive maneuver by a guilt-ridden conscience.*

Ask yourself these questions: Am I absolutely honest in my prayer life? Am I absolutely loving in my prayer life? Am I absolutely unselfish in my prayer life?

Now proceed to confess your sins or shortcomings to God. Be honest about it. Say, "God, You know that I have often claimed to believe in You when I really haven't. But I'm thrilled to know that You love me even though I have my doubts about You at times. I'm glad to know that You want to be my friend, even though You know that I'm not a perfect person. You know I have a tough time loving myself because I"—(and here openly speak out your fears, worries, guilt).

As has often been noted, confession is good for the soul. You will never eliminate the guilt which keeps you from loving yourself until you get it into the open. Until you confess to your guilt, you will continue to rationalize, make excuses and fail to face up to your own sins and shortcomings. They do exist, be sure of that! Reexamination of yourself will lead to feelings of guilt; guilt will lead to confession; confession will lead to genuine repentance. This is the road to being born again, into a new self.

Bill Sands, founder of the Seventh Step Program, which rehabilitates convicts, tells us that the beginning of the change from a "convict mentality" to a "law-abiding mentality" occurs when a convict is willing to admit out loud, "I have been stupid." Bill Sands tells us that the average prisoner does not think he has been wrong. He only feels that he has been unlucky.

Bill says, "I go into prisons wearing my black mohair suit, my alligator shoes, my best silk tie. I sit on the platform and say to these guys in prison, "Hi! How do you like my shoes? What are *you* wearing? How do you like my suit of clothes? What are *you* wearing? Say, you fellas ought to see the bed I sleep in. It's fabulous. White sheets, big pillows, foam rubber mattress. That's living! What kind of beds are *you* sleeping in nowadays? Incidentally fellas, when I get out of here tonight I'm going to go out and have a steak dinner—rich, thick, rare. I'll be listening to soft music with my lovely wife sitting across the table. Then we'll get into my car and we'll drive through the hills to our beautiful home.' "

Then Bill Sands pauses and finally shouts out, "Get smart. Who's stupid? You or me? I obey the laws and I eat good, sleep well and have freedom. You break the laws. You get stuck in this pen. You think you're smart and everybody who obeys all the laws is stupid. Who's stupid, really?"

Deep and lasting change occurs when you express genuine repentance, admitting, "I have been wrong. I am going to change!"

III. POSITIVE AFFIRMATION

Affirmation is the third step to self-love–producing prayer. Now that you have gone through the torturing experience of deeply confessing and pouring out your sins and your guilt, accept God's love and forgiveness. Don't keep on confessing your sins. Don't continue to tell God what a miserable person you are. To continue to do so will only feed the negative self-image you have of yourself. Now is the time to stop repenting and start affirming: "God loves me. God loves me even though I am not perfect. God loves me even though I do not have the faith that I ought to have. This must mean I am a wonderful person."

From this point on, abolish all negative statements from your prayer activity. You can pray yourself into a great and wonderful self-concept, or you can pray yourself into believing you are still a miserable, inadequate, inferior, ineffective person. The Bible says, "God is faithful and just. If we confess our sins God is faithful to forgive us of all of our iniquities." This means that if you have truly exercised the catharsis of confession you are forgiven and clean. Affirm OUT LOUD: "I am God's friend. God loves me. If God has chosen me for His friend I must be a marvelous person."

Probably the hardest assignment in this book will be regularly, vocally, positively to repeat these self-confidence–generating affirmations.

"I can do all things through Christ who strengthens me." I have powers within me that I have not uncovered. I have great potentialities. I can accomplish impossible feats because God and I are working together.

IV. YIELD YOURSELF TO CHRIST

This is the fourth step to self-image–transplanting prayer. Perhaps the most effective prayer ever was uttered by Jesus Christ in the Garden of Gethsemane when He prayed, "My father, all things are possible unto Thee. Let this cup pass from me. Nevertheless not my will, but Thine be done."

You achieve an enormous sense of self-worth when you realize that you are teamed up with God in doing wonderful work in this world. God has a plan for your life. He cannot do anything with you so long as you think that you are worthless, ineffective and unworthy. God can only do great things through self-confident human beings. You build yourself up to self-confidence when you have pursued God, repented of

179

your sins, affirmed His friendship and forgiveness. Now you are ready to yield your confident life to His service.

The real purpose of prayer is to draw you close to God so He can fulfill His will in your life. Many people fail in prayer simply because they use prayer to try to get "what they want, when they want it, the way they want it." Such prayer is doomed to failure.

When you are in a boat and want to move close to shore, you throw the anchor into the sandy beach and pull on the anchor rope until the shore slides under the bow of your boat. What have you really done? You have not moved the beach to the boat; you have moved the boat to the beach. Prayer is designed to draw us close to God; it is not designed to move God to our will. As Frank Laubach reminds us in his great book, *Channels of Spiritual Power*, prayer is not a bucket— it is a fountainhead. Prayer is designed to connect your life to God, that His loving spirit may flow through your life into the lives of others around you. When God is flowing through you to help other human beings, you will have the most enormous sense of self-worth you've ever experienced.

"Lord, show me the person You want to speak to through my life today." A friend of mine recently gave me this simple prayer. I was so impressed with it that I scrawled it on a large piece of paper and taped it to my mahogany-paneled office door. Sitting behind my desk, I can look up and see the prayer scribbled in large letters—"Lord, show me the person You want to speak to through my life today." In the short time that it's been up there, it has already fed my sense of self-worth enormously. After I had put it on the door, I had a telephone call from a young girl in a high school in Fullerton, California. She had a most unusual request. "This com-

180

ing Thursday, Reverend, our junior history class would like to have a minister come in and tell us about the place of Christian faith in modern life. Would you be willing to do it? There are five classes beginning at 8:10 in the morning and concluding at 3:00 in the afternoon. There are over one hundred students in each class. It would be a wonderful opportunity for you to share your faith in God with all of us. But the only day that the school will set aside for this project is Thursday."

I had already reserved Thursday to prepare the initial outline for this book. I was about to explain that I was committed for the day when my eyes looked up and I again read this little prayer—"Lord, show me the person You want to speak to through my life today." Before I realized it, I said, "Okay. I'll be there at 8:10 Thursday morning."

I had one of the greatest days of my whole life! I was able to help many young people who had real spiritual problems. At the end of the day I had the wonderful feeling that God was using my life in an inspiring way. It was one of the outstanding self-loving experiences in my ministry. Through this simple little prayer I had yielded to God's will and had received the greatest reward possible. I really enjoyed living with myself that day!

V. EXPECTING

If your prayer has followed the first four steps—(1) pursuing God, (2) reexamination of self, (3) affirmation of God's forgiveness and love, (4) yielding your self-will to God's will for your life—then you are ready for the fifth step of prayer and can expect great things to happen. Your prayers should continue to be positive. Do not allow your prayer to turn into a crying jag, an anxiety-generating exercise, a worry-feeding talk.

No! You pack power into your prayer by jamming it with expectant thoughts.

"God—I know that You are planning something wonderful."

"God—I don't know how You are going to solve my problem, but I know You have something in mind and I thank You for it."

"God—You are going to use me in ways that I do not know, but I expect that You have something wonderful around the corner!"

I have traveled around the world often enough to know that many people who try to exercise prayer power are doing themselves more harm than good. I have seen people literally crawl in the dust, acting like worms, pouring out their pitiful pleadings to a vague deity. I have heard other people pray with a mourning cry, a wailing and a weeping sing-song voice, with faces long, drawn and anguish-torn. Such prayer is by no means true communion with God. It is the exercise of a neurotic and fearing personality. Health-producing, power-generating, self-love–creating prayer is prayer that is filled with a dynamic spirit of optimism.

If you have approached God honestly and have honestly asked Him to cleanse you of all guilt, if you have affirmed your faith in Him and have yielded yourself to His will, then you have every right to expect that He will do what is best for your life.

This *does not* mean that you can expect a bed of roses,

everything you desire. It *does* mean that you can expect that your life will take on love and meaning. And if there is love and meaning to your life, you will be able to place great, affectionate value on yourself.

The Bible makes it very clear that Christians are soldiers —not tourists in life. We are also servants of God, not house guests.

Pack your prayers with expectancy, and you will begin to believe that you and God together can do great things. You will attempt the "impossible." You will succeed. You will know the great thrill of climbing a mountain! Expect things to happen—and you give life all you've got. If you don't expect things to go right, you will hold back, restrain yourself and produce failure by your own lack of joyful anticipation.

VI. REJOICING COMPLETES THE SELF-IMAGE TRANSPLANT

Pack praise and thanksgiving into your prayer and you will put power into it. Thank God for what He has done and for what He is planning to do. Thank God for the possibilities that you have to be useful and needed in life. Thank God for giving you complete freedom from guilt. Count your many blessings. Name them one by one, and you will be surprised at what the Lord has done. Jam your prayers with statements of positive thinking. Fatigue, depression, despair, defeat will depart from you. Hopefulness, cheerfulness, buoyancy will take over your spirits. Thank God for your problems. They are opportunities in disguise. Thank God you don't know what the future holds for you—it means He's still working on it! Thank God for all of your assets. Think of what you have. Eyes to see? Ears to hear? Fingers? Hands that can write? Thank God that Christ is living in you; that He is loving people through you.

Dr. Henry Poppen is a member of my staff who served for forty years as a dedicated missionary in China. When he celebrated his golden anniversary as a minister, he received this card from a Chinese friend overseas: "Dr. Poppen, we remember you as a mind through which Christ thinks, a heart through which Christ loves, a hand through which Christ works."

Prayer can make you into that kind of person! You will thrill to your new self-image.

XII

LET A WINNER LEAD THE WAY

Now YOU KNOW—nothing is more important to your emotional health than a warm and wonderful feeling of self-worth.

Now YOU KNOW—that unless you develop a devotion to your best self, you will continue to live life on a low level.

Now YOU KNOW—how to build a self-confidence–generating self-esteem that can turn you into a marvelous possibility thinker.

Now

REMEMBER THIS—self-worth is a tenuous property. You can lose it after you have acquired it. Fresh assaults on your newfound self-esteem are sure to come your way.

Prepare now to preserve, protect and polish your self affection. How do you do this? By drawing close to someone who is strong, who can satisfy your deep need for self-dignity.

Here then is your final assignment.

Let a winner lead the way. Find a genuine friend who is strong, secure and serene. In his presence your faltering self-esteem will be renewed. The tragedy is that we are inclined to withdraw from the self-assured person when we begin to lose our self-respect. As the old maxim states, "Birds of a feather flock together." Successful people seek out others who are successful because they believe they are worthy of the valued fellowship of such strong personalities. On the other

185

hand, the person who does not love himself tends to seek those as weak as himself or weaker.

A family whose daughter was a juvenile delinquent moved to California, hoping to separate their daughter from her demoralizing friends. They moved into a fine middle-class community. By the end of the first week in the new high school, their daughter had made new friends. You've guessed it. They were the same kind of delinquent youngsters who used drugs. Why was this? For two reasons: (1) She felt unworthy of the affection of the non-drug users. She felt that their association would have been a judgment upon her. (2) In an effort to salvage a little self-esteem, she had sought out the kind of students who would not condemn, criticize or reject her.

This girl was letting the losers lead her life. Our program of counseling her was directed to building up her self-worth to the point where she believed that she could be loved and respected by people of true worth. To be her companions I elected two young people who themselves had once been on drugs. They were now clean. They understood and accepted her as she was, and welcomed her into their Christian Club. There she was introduced to the greatest person she had ever met, Jesus Christ. He transformed her life.

She learned the exciting facts about His life. *He was born and raised in poverty.* He lived on what we would call the wrong side of the tracks. He had neither a wardrobe nor a residence to which He could point with pride. He never became the confidant of the big shots of His day. He was the classic example of the common man. He belonged to an oppressed minority group—the Jews. Yet He never returned taunts with belligerency. He knew that insults and injustice could either turn Him into a better person—or a worse person. It all depended on Him. Using a positive attitude, He

186

made negative social situations a way to turn Himself into a more sensitive, understanding, compassionate human being.

His family connection was simple and unpretentious. His father was a carpenter. The family lived in the poorest section of the poorly considered village of Nazareth. Yet He was proud of His family. For they were good people.

He held no academic degrees, never traveled more than seventy-five miles from home, published no books, built no marble-columned buildings. His only achievement was the building of a personal character and reputation that would be an inspiration to millions yet unborn. How did He become this kind of a person? By specializing in the building of self-worth in persons that appeared worthless.

How did He build self-love in self-condemning people?

He never called them sinners. Instead He gave them a new self-image, with words such as "You are the light of the world"—"You are the salt of the earth"—"Follow me and I will make you fishers of men"—"Your sins are forgiven"— "If you have faith as a grain of mustard seed, you can say to your mountain—move—and nothing will be impossible to you."

Even His shameful death failed to destroy His strong self-assurance. To be crucified was to die the most ignominious death possible—naked, undraped, exposed in daylight to the stares of men, women and children. To add further insult and indignity, He was hanged in the company of two common thieves. Still He died—as He lived—in dignity. How? By remembering those around Him who had problems, He was first of all concerned about the executioners: how they would hate themselves after the bloody deed was all over. "Father, forgive them, for they know not what they do," He prayed.

His spirit lives on today. He lives to tell you that you too are a wonderful person when you allow yourself to be used by God to save men from self-degradation and help raise them to self-dignity.

In the musical drama *The Man of La Mancha* Don Quixote meets a woman of the streets, a wild, wanton wench named Aldonza. The man of La Mancha stops short, looks at her intently, and announces that she is his lady, whom he will call Dulcinea. She responds with mocking laughter that she is hardly a lady. Still Don Quixote sees the seed of potential greatness and tries desperately to give her a new self-image of the person she really is—if she can believe it. He insists that she is his lady. Angered and hurt, with wild hair flying over nearly naked breasts, she screams that she is only a kitchen maid and a strumpet—nothing. She is Aldonza, not Dulcinea. She runs from the stage as the man from La Moncha whispers again that she is his lady. At the close of the play Don Quixote is dying. He feels he has failed. To his side comes Aldonza-Dulcinea, now lovely in a new gentleness. Confused, he does not recognize this lovely stranger until in a warm voice she tells him that she is his Dulcinea. She has been saved from self-hate and has been taught self-love. She was truly born again.

Sometimes another person can work wonders in your life, in the way Don Quixote finally affected Aldonza. But Jesus Christ will always work miraculous changes if you let Him.

Let me tell you about Vicky, a beautiful young girl from our community whose story illustrates what I mean. She went to college at Berkeley, where she began "dropping acid." Marijuana and LSD became a way of life for her. When her parents asked her to come home for a visit, she agreed with one provision—that she would be able to return to Berkeley and never come home again. I received a telephone call from her parents urging me to talk with her while she was home. The entire family came to my office together, father, mother and daughter. Vicky looked terrible. Her beautiful young face was distorted. Inner tensions, guilt and her hardened attitude had altered her appearance. With sincerity she declared to me, "I have found God in LSD. Every Friday night we have our services. It's beautiful. You don't know what God is like until you've found God in LSD."

"I believe I have found God in Jesus Christ," I replied. "You claim," I continued, "that you have found God in LSD." "Who's right? You or me?" "Let's put God to the test," I suggested. "God is love—do you agree?" She nodded her head approvingly. "Love is helping people," I added. "Do you agree?" She nodded her head again. "How much money have you collected in your LSD services to feed the hungry, to help the crippled, to find a cure for cancer?" I asked. She was silent.

"I must tell you, Vicky," I went on, "because of the spirit of Jesus Christ that lives in the lives of people in this church, we have been able to convert fifty thousand dollars over the past twelve months into help for human beings with problems. The Christian Church has built hospitals, institutions for the blind, the sick and the lame, and provided care for millions of unhappy people."

A sad look of disillusionment began to appear on the face of this young lady.

"Let's all stand, hold hands and pray," I suggested. Father, mother, daughter and I joined hands in a circle. I offered this simple prayer, "Jesus Christ, Your spirit of love lives within my heart. I pray that You will come into the life and heart of Vicky Snapp." As I finished, I saw a tear slide from her eye, and down her cheek. My finger reached over her soft cheek, picking up the wet drop of warm emotion. Holding it before her, I exclaimed, "Vicky! Look what fell out of your eye! Didn't you feel beautiful inside when this tear was forming and falling? This is the deepest and most joyous experience a human being can know. It is religious emotion. It is the movement of a Divine Spirit within you. Christ is coming into your life, Vicky. Let Him come in. Don't be afraid of Him. Nothing good ever dies inside when Christ comes in. Many wonderful things come alive inside of you when Christ comes to live in you. Look at the sky—it's blue. Look at the grass—it's really green. Look at the flowers—they are really red. While you had this high trip which put this beautiful tear in your eye, you were in complete control of yourself. This is reality. It is not artificially induced. It is authentic. The world around you is not distorted or hidden in a psychedelic fog. You can trust this Christ." At that point tears were flowing freely from Vicky's eyes. Jesus Christ had taken control.

Almost immediately her facial expression changed. The narrowing eyes of suspicion and rebellion changed into the round, open, beautiful eyes of a wonderment-struck girl. The face which was formerly tight, tense and older than her years relaxed. Once more the cheeks had the full blossom and the warm rounded shape of a pretty young maiden.

As I write this, two years later, Vicky Snapp is devoting her life to helping people discover that the greatest trip you can take is when you tune into Jesus Christ, who really turns life on! You cannot help loving yourself when He is a part of you.

"Does Christ really change people—in depth?" you may ask. Absolutely! Let me explain the process in a scientific frame of reference. The popular psychiatrist Eric Berne, in his best-selling book, *Games People Play*, explains that every person has at least three ego states. This explains a great deal about behavior, both good and bad. There is the child ego state. To a certain degree we are children all our lives. This explains why many adults act like little children at times, pouting, fighting, screaming. It is an infantile attempt by an adult to achieve self-love. As children we probably had experiences where we "got our way" when we pouted, cried or threw a tantrum. Of course, that doesn't really build self-love, especially in adults.

A second ego state is the parent ego state. Our deep subconscious memory has recorded all of the reactions of our parents that we witnessed or experienced. Many times as we go through life, in facing a problem or experiencing a crisis, we find ourselves acting exactly as our mother or our father would have acted. You may suddenly observe with great surprise your reaction and say to yourself, "Boy, if that wasn't just like my dad (or mother)."

The third is the adult ego state. There are times when you act and react not as a child or as your parents did, but as an independent mature adult. This, according to Berne, is maturity.

However, I believe a fourth ego state is possible. When both your subconscious and your conscious minds are committed deeply, emotionally, intellectually and admiringly to Jesus Christ, a new ego is created within you. You experience the Christ ego state.

There are times in my life, as in other people's lives, when the child comes out in me. There are other times when the parent ego is present. There are times when I react as a mature adult. But there are many other times when I find Christ's Spirit controlling me. Words tumble from my lips that inspire people and surprise me. Those are exalted experiences when I can say with St. Paul, "It is no longer I but Christ who lives in me." An enormous emotion of self-worth obsesses me in that moment of nobility. The key to self-love then may be found in the words of St. Paul, "Let the mind of Christ be in you."

When the Christ ego state becomes a part of you, everything changes because you begin really to love people as well as yourself. There are, Fromm points out, different levels of love: (1) I want you, therefore I love you; (2) I need you, therefore I love you. In both cases, love tends to be selective and conditioned. In these dimensions, love is primarily self-seeking. Love must move to a more rewarding level: (3) You need me, therefore I love you. The problem is that we do not dare to love on this level until we have learned to love ourselves.

When we love ourselves, we want to share ourselves. Only when we are self-assured, self-confident and comfortable with ourselves do we dare to give ourselves to others. It takes great courage to love. For love means involvement, the risk of disappointment, the chance of exposing our intimate life to another person. Only the person who is really deeply self-trusting has the courage to love on this vulnerable level. How can we love ourselves deeply enough to risk sharing ourselves?

The only way I know for this kind of love, which is on the deepest level, to be able to enter and remain in a person's life is for the Spirit of Christ to come into one's life. When Christ's mind becomes a part of your mind, you begin to become a self-trusting, self-loving, self-sharing person. I offer a prayer that can lead you into a new life. Pray this prayer every day for thirty days.

> Christ—here is my brain—think through it.
> Christ—here is my face—glow through it.
> Christ—here are my eyes—look at people through them.
> Christ—here is my heart—love people with it.

To keep your self-love growing and glowing, follow a winner. Read His words. Meet Christ in the Bible. Join the happy Christians in your community church. You will catch His spirit. He will live His life through you. Your life can be a glove with Christ's hand in it. You'll find life is worth living when you find a God worth loving.